GROW INTO YOUR GREATNESS

21 Key Principles to Transform and Access Your Destiny

DR. JERRELL STOKLEY JR.

WESTBOW
PRESS®
A DIVISION OF THOMAS NELSON
& ZONDERVAN

Scripture quotes marked (AMP) are taken from the Amplified Bible (AMP) Copyright © 2015 by The Lockman Foundation, La Habra, CA 90631. All rights reserved. Scripture quotes marked (NKJV) are taken from the New King James Version®. Copyright © 1982 by Thomas Nelson. Used by permission. All rights reserved.

This book is a work of non-fiction. Unless otherwise noted, the author and the publisher make no explicit guarantees as to the accuracy of the information contained in this book and in some cases, names of people and places have been altered to protect their privacy.

WestBow Press books may be ordered through booksellers or by contacting:

WestBow Press
A Division of Thomas Nelson & Zondervan
1663 Liberty Drive
Bloomington, IN 47403
www.westbowpress.com
844-714-3454

Because of the dynamic nature of the Internet, any web addresses or links contained in this book may have changed since publication and may no longer be valid. The views expressed in this work are solely those of the author and do not necessarily reflect the views of the publisher, and the publisher hereby disclaims any responsibility for them.

Any people depicted in stock imagery provided by Getty Images are models, and such images are being used for illustrative purposes only. Certain stock imagery © Getty Images.

ISBN: 978-1-5127-6919-7 (sc)
ISBN: 978-1-5127-6920-3 (hc)
ISBN: 978-1-5127-6918-0 (e)

Library of Congress Control Number: 2016921138

Print information available on the last page.

WestBow Press rev. date: 07/18/2024

Table of Contents

Acknowledgements.. vii

Forward ix

Book Premise xi

Introduction.. xiii

Chapter 1   The Power of Transformation 1

Chapter 2   The Greater Principle 27

Chapter 3   The Acknowledgment 2Principle.................................... 37

Chapter 4   The Prick Principle 45

Chapter 5   The Nourishment Principle 51

Chapter 6   The Response Principle.. 59

Chapter 7   The Vision Principle 69

Chapter 8   The Rooting Principle 77

Chapter 9   The Participation Principle 87

Chapter 10   The Strategy Principle 101

Chapter 11   The Enemy Principle 111

Chapter 12   The Self-Discipline Principle 123

Chapter 13   The Fully Present Principle.. 131

Chapter 14   The Inside/Out Principle... 139

Chapter 15   The Observation Principle... 147

Chapter 16   The Completion Principle 153

Chapter 17   The Relapse Principle 161

Chapter 18   The Structure Principle 169

Chapter 19   The Destiny Principle......................................175

Chapter 20   The Behavior Principle 183

Chapter 21   The Renewal Principle...................................193

Chapter 22   The Testing Principle.....................................199

Chapter 23   The Power of Self-Development.................... 205

About the Author...219

Bibliography..221

Acknowledgements

I would like to thank God for his son Jesus Christ and for every blessing that He has bestowed upon my life by His grace! Lord, without your presence with me each day to lead and guide me, I would not and could not make it through the storms and valleys. Thank you for keeping me in the midst of it all and making your light shine upon me.

I would like to thank my wife of nearly thirty years. Angela, you have been the source of my strength in more ways than you know. I will forever cherish the sacrifice that you have made in being my loving wife and best friend. My dearest love, I would give you the world if it were possible.

I would like to thank my family – each of you. We've all seen some very rough times. I pray that each of you will find joy and peace in Jesus Christ. And that His favor will never fail you.

I would like to thank everyone who reads this book. I pray that your transformation and destiny will be beyond what you expect. I wrote this book so that you can experience exceptional growth and success in life and legacy. Read it carefully. Study it thoroughly. Embrace it fully. And who you desire to be and what you desire to fulfill will all come to pass.

Forward

Grow Into Your Greatness 21 Key Principles to Transform and Access Your Destiny is indeed a power pact, life-changing, guidebook for every person interested in changing, improving, or enhancing his or her life in every area. The techniques and principles displayed and explained in this book are what I call "lifelong enhancement tools" that can be used at every age, stage, and season of life. This book should be found in the personal library and on the office shelves of every dreamer, believer, visionary, entrepreneur, and the like. If you desire to live life to the fullest, aspire to dreams and goals that you have allowed to become silenced by hurt, pain, and distractions, this book has been tailor-made just for you!

Grow Into Your Greatness 21 Key Principles to Transform and Access Your Destiny will get you to those places that you are both quietly and desperately desiring. Apostle Stokley takes you step by step through an amazing journey of change and helps you to face the fears that have plagued you for years and hindered your growth. If you are tired of 'wandering in the wilderness,' going around the same mountains and situations over and over again and coming out the same, this book is for you!

Grow Into Your Greatness 21 Key Principles to Transform and Access Your Destiny will not only help you to discover that change is needed, but it will also encourage and empower you to make the necessary changes to get off of life's merry-go-round and start evolving into the amazing, empowered, unique creation that you were intended to be. After reading this book, you will never be the same. You will refuse to stay a caterpillar and look forward to blossoming into the amazing butterfly that has been within all along! Today begins your day of CHANGE!

- Angela M. Stokley, MBA
President of Angela Inspires
Co-Founder of Covenant Grace Church

Book Premise

Grow Into Your Greatness is written based on the premise that everyone has a divine greatness inside of them. The Open Bible Sense Lexicon describes great as remarkable, out of the ordinary in degree, magnitude, or effect. Everyone has an exceptional calling and gifting. The greatness expressed in this book is not a greatness to be attained by wealth, power, fame, or materialism. It is a greatness obtained through becoming the most extraordinary version of yourself. The person that you are predestined to be.

For the purposes of this book true greatness is only obtained through humility and servitude to others. Matthew 20:25-28 says, "Jesus called them to him and said, "You know that the rulers of the Gentiles lord it over them, and their great ones exercise authority over them. It shall not be so among you. But whoever would be great among you must be your servant, and whoever would be first among you must be your slave, even as the Son of Man came not to be served but to serve, and to give his life as a ransom for many.

Daniel 6:3a says this, "Daniel distinguished himself above the governors and satraps, because an excellent spirit was in him." Luke 1:15, speaking of John the Baptist says, "For he will be great before the Lord. And he must not drink wine or strong drinks, and he will be filled with the Holy Spirit, even from his mother's womb. True greatness is an act of God's spirit transforming us into the image of Christ and fulfilling His mighty acts in the earth. Greatness is a growth process that requires change! We can't step into it. We must transform into it!

The only decision you have to make is whether you are going to be a "master of change" or a "victim of change." Are you going to be a creator of circumstances or a creature of circumstances? ...It will be one or the other, but the impact of change will be forced upon you, whatever you do.
                                        -Brian Tracy, Success Guru, and Author

Your level of maturity is measured by how well you handle change...maturity is measured by one's capacity to respond effectively to the unexpected.
                                        -Dr. Myles Monroe, Author, and Senior Pastor

The first step towards change is awareness. If you want to get from where you are to where you want to be, you have to start by becoming aware of the choices that lead you away from your desired destination.
                                        -Darren Hardy, Author, and Publisher of Success Magazine

Introduction

Unavoidable Growth & Change

Here is the reality. Everyone experiences change and growth. Start making a difference in how you approach change and growth today. Your focus cannot be on the past but on the present and the future. I once read a statement from Theodore Roosevelt that motivated me to take charge of my life. It said, *"Do what you can, with what you have, right where you are."* Grow Into Your Greatness 21 Key Principles to Transform and Access Your Destiny will teach and guide you through ways to master your growth, achieve greatness, experience God's divine process to destiny, initiate the changes you need to make, and pursue God whole-heartedly. This book will serve as a compass to guide you through the phases of change and greatness in your life and legacy. You will better understand how to use your mind and words to create self-discipline, mental clarity, and new habits to succeed at anything that you desire! There is nothing that will be unachievable for you after reading this book.

Change is not always a matter of uncontrollable external forces. In fact, change is also a method of internal strategic thought and action. Above all, change is a biological, physiological, spiritual, and holistic part of life. *Change is unavoidable!* If you knew something catastrophic or of significant influence was about to take place, would you want to be prepared or know what to do to have the right response? I am sure that you would. I know that I would. Here is a fact: change is happening every day. It can either be at the root of your personal and professional catastrophe or at the helm of your sailboat of success. Either outcome is up to you. Something significant is about to happen to you!

As you live your dreams, attempt to fulfill goals, develop vision, build a loving family, marry the person of your dreams, cast your biggest career net, meet the challenges, conquer mountains, and surf the waves of success, change will secure your seat in the winner's row or lower you into the bowels and abyss of failure. You must either be a change agent or roll with the change agent that is currently operating in your life if you want to win!

Responsible People Grow

Change agents are people, circumstances, misfortunes, opportunities, and the like that come along at calculated and often unpredictable moments and can cause life-altering results. One of my mentors, Jim Rohn said, *"You must take personal responsibility. You cannot change circumstances, the seasons, or the wind but you can change yourself-that's something you have charge of."* I call these types of circumstances "agents of change." You have probably experienced an agent of change in your life. For example, an unplanned pregnancy or a lay-off from work is an agent of change. A sudden illness or successful career move is an agent of change. A community destroying tornado or a surprise monetary gift from a loving friend is an agent of change.

A spiritual awakening or a failed economy is an agent of change. Every circumstance plays a role in producing change around us. And I believe that some changes we experience are divinely assigned. Thus, life seems to make us stronger through the process of enduring change.

Change agents force you to "go with the flow" or adapt and conform to wisdom. They thrust you into a cycle of ups and downs as well as new discoveries about yourself. Change agents can even take you on the thrill ride of a lifetime. For example, meeting the person of your dreams; building your first home from the ground up; or even landing a top position in a firm that you thought was a little bit out of your skillset or educational level. Allow me to tell you about my change agent that suddenly thrust me into a life transforming season of new discoveries and amazing success. His name is Jared Stokley, and he is my youngest son. At a time in our society when families are so divided and separated based on generational mindsets, who would have imagined that at 45-year-old father with twenty years of investing in career moves and game-changing attempts could gain life-changing insight from his then 19-year-old son, who at the time was a sophomore in college? Well, I didn't imagine it, but it happened.

My Story

It happened one Wednesday night immediately following Bible study. I dismissed the service and began to fellowship with the congregation. After some time passed, I moved to the back of the sanctuary to talk with the audio technicians. Soon I noticed someone standing beside me. I turned to face the shadow of a person to give them my attention. There he was, looking like his mother, and staring in my direction. His eyes had a glaze over them as if he were in a trance. He had that look a person has when they appear to be looking at you, but they are looking past you. This is what he was doing. He was looking in my direction, but I could tell he was not looking at me. His focus was somewhere else. He called out to me, "Dad." "Yes, Jared," I said. "Dad, I feel like God has given me something to say to you." I thought to myself, ", Boy, what are you talking about?" I will admit I was taken aback. I felt very unsettled about his facial expression and his frozen stance. Honestly, I was kind of afraid. Again, I thought to myself in an arrogant tone, "What could God have told my son to tell me?" As he continued staring off in a trance he said, "God wants you to change!" "Change," I thought. "He wants you to be humbler," he said. He continued, "If you don't change, you won't go to the next level of your destiny. God will not allow you to get there. He told me these things because He knows how much you love me and that you would receive this from me." I thought, "What in the world is going on?" I was blown away. Speechless. I didn't know what to say or do, but I pondered his words carefully.

Anyone who knows me knows that I am a destiny and purpose fanatic of sorts. I used to live and breathe for destiny until I learned that living and breathing for The Father is the ultimate quality of life! I looked at my son in total shock. I was unsettled and extremely curious. At the time of his "divine pronouncement" I was doing everything I had learned to grow and to develop.

I was practicing servant leadership, humility, stewardship, and success. I was already in tune with some habits and beliefs that I needed to improve and fine-tune. I was practicing ways to improve both privately and publicly. I could not imagine any more changes that I could manage.

Yet, when my son said this to me, the weight and reality that my destiny and success hinged upon change gave me courage to do the one thing that I had been procrastinating to do for years. I was so afraid of this for many reasons. Yet, instantly, I knew what I needed to do to change. Destiny was on the line. And I needed to pay the price.

My Desperate Need for Therapy

When you have done everything but the right thing, the necessary thing, is the only answer. The necessary thing is often the act that you fear the most, the one that you know will work but will also hurt the most. I knew that there was one thing that I needed, yet I was fearful to undertake it. I had developed self-limiting beliefs about this one decision. Let me tell you why before I tell you what. In my circles of influence, the thing that I needed to do was seldom discussed and often ridiculed. It was a shame. What I am about to disclose was and still is considered by some as forbidden public territory. This topic for some infamous reason is one that can only be discussed in private.

Here it is. I am laying it all out there on the line. I needed help. I needed help from someone who could teach me to master my behavior and emotions, and to live victorious over past failures, hurt, mistakes, and abuse. Yes, abuse. I need counseling. I needed trauma therapy. I was too easily triggered. The following day after Bible study, a Thursday morning, I got on the phone and called a therapist. There I said it. Yes, that is right! A therapist. I did it and I am now saying it to everyone, "Get the help you need!" Open up and discuss your need for help. Cry aloud and stop being ashamed and squirming into a dark corner of weakness and internal turmoil because of what people may say or think. Sometimes, the only way to change is to get some help!

Soon, I began the process of going to therapy for all the things inside of me that were broken, all the habits I needed to change, all the areas that spirituality did not cure, and, more importantly, the growth I needed to be successful at the next stage of my life. My son was not wrong, and neither was God. I was hurting and broken. I was what is called a functional professional but hiding my instability for many years. Privately, I struggled with my brokenness yet publicly I performed with excellence and perfection. I was hiding my weaknesses. What about you? Are you hiding yours? Do you need therapy to change?

Can this book be an opportunity for you to come out of hiding? Is it possible that by simply reading this introduction your thinking has begun to change? Are you ready to open up and find help for your broken soul, heart, and state of being? Listen to your heart, your friends, or your spouse about the change you may need. Maybe they are right. Maybe they see, sense, and know that your awesomeness is clouded by your ego. Acknowledge the deeper voice within that is reasoning with you about your unhealthy or unfruitful self-limiting beliefs.

I knew that if I invested my all into this therapeutic process in the exact measure in which I did everything else, it would transform my life for the good and launch me into a new stage of healing, career, and purpose. Growing into greatness requires the grace to address our need to get better. We often find the grace to help others wounds while denying ourselves much needed compassion and healing.

I have concluded that God was doing me a favor. He loves me enough to send a message through my nineteen-year-old son. God knew that I would listen *and* act. Such is the mystery of God. He knows what we need and how to get it to us. The message was clear. God loves me and wants me to achieve my deepest desires and dreams. My act of faith was to embrace the process with tenacity, hope, and strategy. My faith in His plan has paid off tremendously.

My obedience to seek change and help through therapy prepared me to achieve so much more in my life. Couseling gave me the added insight, mastery of behavior, and clarity of thought necessary to gain God's trust for the next dimension. The deep examination and rebuilding process stabilized me for a more prosperous stage of my life and career. The deeper success was not in the therapy. Instead, it was in the act of change that I committed toward the therapy. As it has been for me, so shall it be for you! If you are willing to make your necessary change, good change, you will find favor with God!

The Dividends of Change

If you change, it will pay off. Change pays dividends. Over time I began to recognize a new element of destiny and purpose for my life. I was intrigued and began pursuing this new path with joy and excitement. Then it clicked in my thoughts. The "ah ha moment" occurred. I remember thinking, "I'm in a new path of destiny and purpose. God trusts me with greater!" As time progressed, I dove into reading the latest personal development and performance improvement books on the market that also reflected my biblical worldview. Christians are often too spiritual to find value in any reading other than the Bible. The Bible does not give instructions on how to cook, pressure was a house, or file taxes. We need to embrace other profitably material to advance our knowledge. So, I increased the number of transformational programs to which I subscribe.

I completed a high-intensity peak performance course by one of the top Success Mentors in the marketplace. I traveled to attend conferences by some of the leading minds in America and abroad. I reshaped my personal business enterprise and launched new products and services. My self-concept grew healthier. I learned proven strategies to achieve my highest level of growth and success. I acquired mentors at the level in which I aspired to achieve. I wrote myself a new internal story. My marriage began to flourish. Over time, my son noticed the growth. In one conversation, he said, "Dad, I can really see a difference in you." So, the most important people around me became happier. The most important areas of my life became more functional and successful.

The decision to make the hardest changes in my life birthed the most fulfilling journey. Changing was the most significant thing that happened in my life. I grew into greatness that thrust my career in a more positive and successful direction. This one area of growth toward greatness was more significant than anything I had done over the past fifteen years.

I am now practicing new habits for success and am deeply engulfed in changing and becoming the person that I need to be. We often have to become a better version of self to live successfully at the next level of career, family, and future. I am grateful for my son's spiritual growth, beliefs, and personal walk with God. Because of his intimacy with God, he willingly and lovingly relayed the message of God's words to his father and pastor.

The experience totally changed my life. I am thankful to God for what He has done through that one moment. God opened my eyes and is helping me to make the changes I need to make in life. Since that night, I have been on a lifelong journey. I am living more fulfilled and more successful. I am achieving more goals, coming out of old habits, and evolving mentally, behaviorally, professionally, and personally into the greatest person I can ever become. So, what is my goal in authoring this book besides wishing everyone to have my growth experiences?

My goal in authoring this book is to help you become the greatest, most successful person that you can be through a few simple acts of change. How can the slightest change of habit significantly change your life? The answer lies within your willingness to investigate, discover, and engage in growing your greatness.

Real change always produces one great challenge – how. Grow Into Your Greatness *21 Key Principles to Transform and Access Your Destiny*, will carry you through the rough terrain of mastering your behavior and thoughts to get you there. Remember, there is more unique greatness inside of you. There are unchartered waters of your personality, gifting, and anointing for you to sail. There are unfulfilled dreams in you waiting to on a worthy push them out. It is time to shift into the next growth-gear. This is the season to live like you have never lived before. It is time to triple your productivity, intensify your vision, and ramp up your adventure through the act of change! I cannot wait to hear about how adopting these twenty-one principles grew you into your greatness. Success is worth it!

Honoring Success?

We often spend so much time honoring the success of others. We watch their reality shows, subscribe to their social media, enroll in their programs, buy their products, and give to their mission. And there is nothing wrong with that. The challenge is to dispense more of yourself honoring your own success. Outside of a relationship with God, your purest form of joy comes through personal achievement. Whatever that is. Be it family, friends, finances, career, spirituality. Honor your success with more value, time, and attention and you will draw from deeper wells of joy. If you could make one change today, at this very moment, that would provide you with your destiny, what would it be? Did you come up with an answer? If so, is the answer original, made up of your core beliefs? If you answered this question truthfully, then it is time to stop limiting your success.

There is untapped talent and potential inside of you. You are a 'gold mine' of ideas, vision, and opportunities. The cure for diseases, a strategy for new architectural designs, a plan for solving world hunger, a curriculum for mentally challenged learners, a design for the latest fashion, are often caged inside someone creative ability until they grow into their greatness. Joel Osteen, author, and pastor wrote, *"So much of success or failure in life begins in our minds and is influenced by what we allow ourselves to dwell on."* (Your Best Life Now, 2004) When you fail to believe in yourself, you are left with doubt and insecurities about your identity and ability. More simply put, you do not know who you are and what you are capable of doing. You lack the confidence and self-esteem to initiate courageous acts, launch deeper into purpose and begin the process of much needed change. There are few achievements more stimulating in life than recognizing who you are. Think about that for just a moment. Try to answer this question with absolute clarity within ten seconds. Who are you? Not your name or your occupation. Who are YOU? Maybe you don't know. Okay, take a moment, relax your mind, and answer the question. Do it now. Then, come back to this book!

Did you answer the question in ten seconds or less? Did it take you longer? You should be so in tune and convinced about who you are that ten seconds is more than enough time to articulate it to yourself. We can't grow if we don't know what to address. Better yet, what God is attempting to heal or build in us. No worries. You are reading the right book to get you there! Let's hang around this point. Did the question challenge your honesty? What about understanding who you are? Did you struggle to answer this question clearly, specifically, and fully? If so, you have no recourse but to read on.

Did the question scare you? Did it humble you? Did your response surprise you? It is your destiny to uniquely impact the world as only you can. Without the full expression and manifestation of your destiny, some problems in the world will not get solved. There will be people who will never grow past certain circumstances or even believe certain truths unless you become the uniquely great person that you are prewired by God to be. The only thing that you need now is a proven 'greatness growth' process. You are great! Greatness (the ability to achieve unlimited status, influence, prosperity, and legacy) is yours!

Self-Significance Begins Within

Your place in society is significant because you are significant. Significance denotes importance, noteworthiness, or weight. The planet is made up of billions of people; yet there is absolutely no one, single, solitary soul on the planet identical to you. And there never will be. Your thoughts are uniquely yours. Your dreams are uniquely yours. Your passions are uniquely yours. Your creativity is uniquely yours. And your destiny is uniquely yours. Do not spend the rest of your life shopping around for the energy and excitement from someone else's dream, passion, thoughts, creativity, voyage, or journey. Prophet Jeremiah had to be assured by God of the significance bottled up inside of him. He says of Jeremiah, "Before I formed you in the womb I knew you before you were born I set you apart. I appointed you as a prophet to the nations." (Jeremiah 1:5)

Jeremiah had no idea of his significance. He needed revelation. Revelation happens when God chooses to reveal what is hidden to logic, history, pain, or pedigree. Like Jeremiah, there was a time that I did not know my significance. I did not believe I had the potential to author books, mentor, teach, or be a successful entrepreneur. Now, I live so purposefully and energetically because God granted me revelation through His Word and servants. I learned that I couldn't just step into greatness. But I could grow into it.

Change unlocked my thinking. The Bible, the most acclaimed wisdom, and spiritual books of all times, says, "As a man thinks in his heart so is he." (Proverbs 23:7) Change gave me a greater vision of destiny. Change helped me to tell myself a uniquely outrageous and exceptional internal story. We all have an internal story that we tell ourselves over and over and over again. It is the compilation of truths and falsehoods that have been ingrained in you from childbirth until today. It is the story that you repeat in your head when opportunities and or challenges arise. It is the combination of words and descriptive images that appear and sound off in your mind and thoughts as you go about day-to-day. Your internal story is made up of both truth and lies, tragedies and triumphs, tribulations, and troubles. All you need now is a radical turning point.

You may be reading this book because you are either improving your internal story, challenging your internal story, or maybe even rewriting your internal story altogether. Regardless of your reason, growth is necessary for you to achieve your absolute most awesome and fulfilling success story. Once I changed, my willingness to adapt to new ways of thinking and applying myself was unlocked. Every level of success I have experienced and every measure of opportunity I have gained has been a result of making necessary changes and adapting to change in my life. My resistance to do what I needed to do or start over and reinvent myself slowly vanished. I began to enjoy the development and growth of the new me-the person I was destined to be.

A Foundation of Honesty

Maybe you are thinking that change is not a challenge for you. If so, let me ask you a few questions. Are there any unfulfilled dreams in you? If so, why? Do you have a nagging feeling that a part of you is withering away? Are you settling because you know there's more but afraid to explore your next? Have you apologized and reconciled your relationship with a loved one whose presence you still miss? Have you taken that fearful, audacious step towards growing your business? Do you still fear what others think about you? These are the questions that expose our honesty. Honesty is so critical to putting the microscope on our areas of growth and change.

If you have failed to take the steps toward your most frightening goal, deliver on the most important promise, show up in spite of insecurities, or bring the fight for your dreams and purpose, then I must break the news to you. Here it is! You have not been honest with yourself about change. You are a candidate for change! We all have a need to continue to become better. Honesty is a necessity to get us there!

It starts with acknowledging the need to change and accepting personal responsibility for the pursuit of growing into our greatness. If you can think of one episode or situation in your life, dramatic or otherwise that you have not healed from, overcome, conquered or forgiven, then you need to know what the power of change can do for you. If you have one destiny-oriented goal that you have not achieved, then you need to know what the power of change can do for you and how it can impact your life story. If you have been thrusted into an unforeseen circumstance that is either unfavorable or too important to fail at, then you need to experience the power of mastering change.

Time is a dressmaker specializing in alterations.
-Faith Baldwin, Author

For as we know — and I can't repeat it enough — the only certain thing about life is change…To deny the realities of change in our lives is to pretend that the forces of gravity won't pull the ripe apple from the tree.
-Bishop T. D. Jakes, Author, and Producer

Chapter 1

The Power of Transformation

Success Mentor and Author Tony Robbins writes, *"Change is inevitable. Progress is optional."* Wherever you are in your career, relationships, goals, spirituality, pursuits, and dreams are a direct outcome of your ability or inability to change. Transformation is metamorphic. It is a process where we are different in radical or subtle ways. Radical change is not always welcomed but often necessary. Sometimes to get closer to our authentic self we have to become radically different. The greater we expand in growth, the more our capacity for new. Transformation has the power to create a new you. I would imagine that's why Romans 12:2a says, "Be not conformed to this world, but transformed (radically altered...my added emphasis) by the renewing of your mind." Change is universal. And when it is radical its' impact can be global. Consider how AI (artificial intelligence) has unsettled the global marketplace. That's a magnanimous change. Why? Transformation is the fuel for innovation, expansion, increase, success, and growth. Without change the world would cease to advance. Without change our private life would dissolve into boredom and archaism. Growth of knowledge and skill has brought you this far. Growth in compassion and truth builds intimate relationships. As we are willing to transform we harness the power to form new habits.

As the old saying goes, "We all have room for improvement." The challenge is finding the honesty, determination, and strategy to get there. It begins with this truth. Your pain threshold for failing to change must be greater than your pain threshold for succeeding at change. In other words, the painful cost of failing must be greater than the painful cost of succeeding. Furthermore, the reward of succeeding must be greater than the pain of the process. You can harness all the power necessary to change any circumstance in your life. You do not have to settle for any unfavorable outcome.

Change has transformed the world. Change delivers consistently, time and time again. Change matures an adolescent boy into a stunning, responsible man. Change transforms thoughts and ideas into mind-blowing, history making realities. Change can bring out the inner beauty of everyone and everything it touches. Think of the good changes in your life. Maybe you have experienced a change of mind that opened doors to greater dreams and imagination. Maybe you have experienced physical change, and you are the ideal picture of health and physical fitness. If so, how did the change in physical appearance impact your confidence, self-concept, love life or dating life? Maybe you have relocated into the ideal home or community and now you are creating a warm and peaceful family life. Maybe you have re-enrolled in school or have gone back for certification or even your GED. Change turns what was not into what now is.

Inspired by Change

Inspiration Change can be inspiring, motivational, and life altering. Change is either intentional, natural, or forceful. What if your next act of change, big or small, could catapult you into the dream life, success path, physical fitness, educational level, company position, business growth, spiritual realm, life-long pursuit, or even political path that you have always desired? Would you make changes to grow in your destiny? Can you champion the necessary transformation in your life that has been presented before you or even prodding at you? You may wonder why there are so many questions. My goal is to create a series of "ah ha" moments that create significant trails of discovery. The more discovery you experience the more inspiration you will possess.

Discovery is important because when we discover something new it inspires us with joy to act. Acting out of joy carries us further than acting out of duty. Did you know that feelings of inspiration releases dopamine, endorphins, and serotonin? This trifecta can stimulate the brain body chemistry in astounding ways. This is why motivational speakers are so charismatic and magnetic. They inspire. We respond. Dopamine creates feelings of happiness and optimism. Imagine that. Just a few changes here and there in your life could create more joy. Endorphins are like opiates. They relieve pain, fuel exercise, and put us in a happy mood. Serotonin impacts overall mood and well-being. When we are inspired by change we become an all-around happier person with more drive to achieve greatness.

We all have areas in which we need to improve or change. Yet, we do not all understand the inspiration from achieving the growth we need. Mastering change can prevent regret, quitting, depression, stress, and disease. Mastering change can prevent the guardians of the old paradigms of business, leadership, government, religion etc. from destroying and denying emerging new leaders, concepts, and ideas. Your personal world will flow seamlessly when you allow growth to inspire you. Your state of emotions will remain healthy. Your life pursuit will come to pass. I recall being inspired to go back to college in my thirties while raising four children. It was tough. However, every semester that I completely fueled my inspiration to finish. One act of transformation often builds the mindset to easily endure the cost of the next. Speaking of enduring costs, when I first enrolled back into college, we were rebounding from financial collapse. Our family business went bankrupt. We were basically homeless. We lost everything. Literally. God caused my path to cross with a homeowner who was renting a fixer upper. If it were not for this gentlemen's grace to allow me to fix the house up as a downpayment and first months' rent, my wife and four children would have all been at the shelter with me. So, I needed all the inspiration I could to grow into the man that I needed to be in that season of my life. The serotonin, dopamine, and endorphins that I received from the inspiration of every change we concurred built confidence in a brighter day ahead.

Steward Time

A common complaint that I hear from people who are stalled in their destiny and greatness is that they don't have time. But if I ask them for their smart device, I can scroll down their social media timeline and texts and show them just how much time they have. If I looked at their bank statements and logged in the number of times they ate out or their plethora of subscriptions, I could show them how much time they are wasting. As a poor steward of time you will come to ruins, defeat, and fail at the success story designed for your life. But, if you succeed in your stewardship of time by investing time wisely into your goals, dreams, and growth, you can conquer your world! How valuable is time to you? You must be able to answer this question with extreme clarity. Proverbs 90 draws a correlation between time and wisdom. It says, "So teach us to number our days that we may get a heart of wisdom." (Psalm 90:2). We need wisdom in how to use time because life is just a vapor and then its' gone. Time is germane for destiny and greatness. And we don't have any to waste. So, let's get moving and steward time to our greatest advantage.

If you place the value of time behind the value of money, success, or relationships, you will miss the bigger picture. For example, without time there is no production of money. Without time, there is no space or development of relationships. Without time, there is no life. Without time, there is no engagement of affairs and business that leads to success. Time is one of the most valuable assets that you possess. Time is a dynamic part of your human assets. Your human assets are directly linked to your profitability, livelihood, and destiny. When you run out of time, that means that you are dead. Dead people don't invest stock, marry, or post on social media. The Apostle Paul writes in Ephesians, "Look carefully then how you walk, not as unwise but as wise, make the best use of time, because the days are evil." (Ephesians 5:15-16)

Time is one of the most powerful forces on the planet. It is eternally active in your life and mine. Setting the clock up an hour gives us an additional hour of sunlight. People see this as more time to enjoy life, adventure, and success. Symbolically, when we value time, we use it to spring forward into new ideas, complete much needed tasks, and learn new skills for success. The new season brings new life, new birth, and new discovery. It helps you to know when to set your clock back an hour in the fall because the old season has passed away. In the fall, we lose an hour of sunlight. Some even say an hour of sleep. Symbolically, it is time to rest. The time-change relationship if valued, will indicate your specific season of rest. Stewarding time keeps you aligned with opportunities to act and move in the direction of greatness.

You will be in tune with the necessary time of refreshing, renewal, and restoration. You will honor the changes in life that reflect the need to pull away from the hustle and bustle and find solace on peaceful shores. Once you develop the mastery of the time, you will be relentless in your pursuit of growing into your greatness. Everything about your biology and psychology is designed to respond to time.

Your body is set on autopilot to respond to the changes in time, seasons, age, atmosphere, everything. You are wired for change. You are in tune with the universe and the world of which God has graced you to be a part. Release yourself to the flow of time and the pursuit of change so that you will be where you should, doing what you should and how you should. If you train for mind in the direction of your change and growth, your body will respond the same. In manufacturing, there is a process known as the time and motion study. A time and motion study are a careful examination of time required, and the nature of each worker's movements to complete a task or a series of tasks for the purpose of determining how to make them more efficient and productive.

This process vets whether time and motion are directly connected. When workers are not producing the necessary activity in the time allotted to achieve the goal, employers have to develop new strategies and technology. Otherwise, production becomes a waste of time and valuable energy which equates to financial deficits. The time and motion study are applicable to life in general. When we are not producing toward destiny with the time allotted we are wasting time and energy. Thus, we are creating destiny deficits. Deficits that only God can nudge us to adjust by infusing new growth strategies like trouble, test, and challenges in an effort to get us to act. Thus, whenever time calls, requires, invites, or forces you to change, you answer the call because you understand the direct connection between time and growth. Now is the time to grow. This book is your revelation from God. It is your prophetic proclamation to step out on faith and walk on the waters of change. Though thunderous and dreadful at times, you must act. And quickly. King Solomon, known as the wisest man, that ever lived, once wrote, "For everything there is a season, and a time for every matter under heaven." (Ecclesiastes 3:1) Something that you're believing God for right now requires that you first grow to gain it. However, investment is always tied to value.

Value Time

There are years of study on time management that has resulted in a great deal of information useful for advancing workplace productivity. However, the latest discoveries in time-management suggest that managing time is impossible. Because time cannot be manipulated or adjusted to fit our schedule or lifestyle. The latest discovery has then defaulted to self-management. The results suggest that we can only manage self or our activities within any frame of time. Time-management concepts have now become self-management truths. Self-management requires you to practice self-discipline. The more disciplined you are or become, the more you can produce and achieve within a frame of time. Develop exceptional self-discipline and your entire life will change in the direction of your exceptional and hopeful future. Self-discipline means that one must intentionally control their focus, behaviors, and heart posture in order to possess the appropriate response. This requires both growth in spirit and growth in mindset.

Self-discipline or self-control which ever settles best with you, is not a new concept. It is as engrained in human development as the Bible is to religion. As a matter of fact, Proverbs wisely teaches that, "A man without self-control is like a city broken into and left without walls." (Proverbs 25:28).

Time significantly influences how we associate value with things. We value antiques and relics because of the time associated with them. In the marketing field, there is a law called the Law of Leadership. Al Ries and Jack Trout state in their book *The 22 Immutable Laws of Marketing* that the basic issue in marketing is creating a category in which you can be first. This is the Law of Leadership: It is better to be first than it is to be better. It is much easier to get into the mind first than to try to convince someone you have a better product than the one that came first.

Let me simplify this to you by asking you the question, "Do you remember your first love?" I am quite sure that you do. First Loves possess a magical way of stealing our heart. They fill us with inspiration to live and cause our emotions to come alive in a way we have never experienced. What is the key? Timing. They may not turn out to be our best love, just our first. Because they were the first to love us in a new way, their passion and presence is forever stained in our hearts and minds. Regardless of how many loves we have after the first love, the first typically has the grandest presence-forever. This elementary example is a basic rendition of proof that timing changes everything. Alignment with the right timing is most beneficial when organic. The more natural our rhythm is with appointed times, which many refer to as 'the right time,' the more in tune we tend to be with the changes that follow. Ecclesiastes 3:11a says, "He (God) has made everything beautiful in its time." When we instinctively act in aligned time with God, then we see beauty of God's timing. So, welcoming change in our heart and mind must become a natural modus operandi – Latin for our "mode of operation." So, seek to be instinctive, organic, and natural.

Instinctive Change

Mark Twain, American Author, and Inventor once said, "In the Spring, I have counted 136 kinds of weather in 24 hours." The process of initiating change, aligning with change, and adapting to change has to become second nature for you to remain happy and successful. It must become your second nature. It must become so ingrained and instilled in you that it happens naturally. Nature always has and always will produce change. The course of all nature has been divinely set. Nothing has been nor will be able to stop the sun nor the moon from rising. Nothing has nor ever will stop the seasons from changing. They change and obey the direct command of God. Psalm 74:16-17 says of God's power over nature, "The day is Yours; the night also is Yours; You have the prepared light and the sun. You have set all the borders of the earth; You have made summer and winter." (NKJV) A deeper dive into God's power of nature is revealed in Matthew 8:23-27, the disciples encountered a storm with fierce wind while Jesus was asleep in the lower parts of the boat. Once the disciple awakened him, He rebuked the wind, and it stopped blowing at His command.

Nothing living stays the same. It changes naturally. This is referred to as organic change. Natural change implies being systematically wired to respond and develop at the appropriate time and in the appropriate way. Your body changes naturally with age. Thus, change is a reality of nature. Adapting this mindset and skillfully transferring this concept into every area of life drives exponential growth! You cannot fail to sense and respond productively to whatever change is necessary to achieve your goals and dreams when you know with conviction that change is natural! And that change must come and will come.

The Rhythm of Change

Many may fail to be successful because they misunderstand the rhythm of change. Companies, technology, medicine, knowledge, anything with or driven by life is in rhythm with change. Change is deeply woven into the fibers of everything in our existence. Yet we often get comfortable in remaining the same. The absolute best way to fail in life is choosing comfort over rhythm of change. Marriages change, movements change, missions change, methods change, minds change, there is nothing living that stays the same. Neither will you! In order acquire happiness, success, and destiny you must be willing to shift with the changes that benefit and breathe life into you and what you are seeking to achieve. Adapt to the rhythm of change in your life. It is a cargo ship commuting you across the massive sea of development so that you can dock in destiny on time.

Dr. Myles Monroe, in his book *The Principles and Benefits of Change* identifies that there are four types of change in which we experience. These four changes are inevitable and there is absolutely no way around them. The four types of change that we all experience are change that happens to us, change that happens around us, changes that happen within us, and changes that initiate. The last is often the hardest if you ask me. Why? Self-initiated change, which we will discuss in a later chapter, requires more willpower, focus, and optimism than other-initiated change. Self-initiated change is often a matter of choice. Other-initiated changes often leave us with no choice. It is forceful. As a result, we adapt or suffer the consequences. Take time in this season of your life and identify if you are in the rhythm of change. If you are not in the rhythm, map a strategy that is built upon prayer, wisdom, vision, and SMART goals. Then, you will find the rhythm that you need to break into a new flow toward your greatness.

Finding Opportunity in Change

Darren Hardy, Success Mentor, Author, and Entrepreneur wrote, "Your life is the product of your moment-to-moment choices." Several benefits of change are new life, growth, and opportunity. The key to identifying them is practicing being 'fully present.' This equates to monitoring your surroundings for open doors and problems that you can solve. It's impossible to be 'fully present' when you are living out old paradigms and antiquated culture. When we live in the past, trauma, pain, and unbelief we narrow the path of exceptionalism and fall short of our "next." We must not simply lethargically show up but rather energetically participate. When we do all types of opportunities materialize. *Greatness requires that things at your next level begin to materialize before you arrive.* Because slight manifestations of next super-charge your inspiration and set your dopamine and serotonin on overflow. And when you are fighting against the winds of rejection and denial, you need as much happy feelings and added energy as you can muster.

Create change in your life and the new you will arise. There is nothing like the rush of energy and excitement that comes from a new opportunity or experience that moves you in the direction of your dreams. Many people run from change. Yet, change should be an exploration for new life, growth, and opportunity. In studying the lives of many successful businesspeople, I have found that it was the little adjustments and changes in their thoughts and habits that led to destiny, legacy, and prosperity. Just imagine what doors might swing wide open if you choose to make small adjustments of change. I can guaranteed that over time your will grow closer and closer to your goals, dreams, and vision. Here is the revelation. Run toward change and not away from change. Maybe you are asking 'what difference can small adjustments make?' In his book *The Compound Effect*, Darren Hardy communicates the compounding effect i.e., rate of multiplied success that can happen as you engage the small change process.

After interviewing and studying the lives of the world's most successful people as well as practicing what he found in his own life, Darren discovered that small, daily choices will shape actions until they become habits. The more you practice successful habits, the more they will become permanent. Change is sometimes necessary to get to the rewarding habits that yield the highest return over time. Darren says, *"Eliminate sabotaging habits and instill the needed, positive habits, and you can take your life in any direction you desire, to the heights of your greatest imagination."* The gold nuggets in his discovery are "eliminating and instilling." They are dance partners. When or if you choose to eliminate apathy and indecision, you must in return instill new habits and learn them well. This requires taking action. Later, we will explore the massive action that you must engage. Tony Robbins, Author, and Peak Performance Coach to millions said, and I quote, *"Your decisions shape your destiny. The future is what you make of it. Little everyday decisions will either take you to the life you desire or to disaster by default."* My friend, this is a great juncture in this reading to begin flowing with the rhythm of this message and maybe what you are sensing from God through it. There is a rhythm in this section of the book that has the power to move you forward. Do you feel it? Can't you sense it? Your time is now! And when you make that mental shift, that you're apprehensively pondering a new version of you will soon emerge!

Emerge in Change

Stephen Covey, in his book The Seven Habits of Highly Effective People, relates to a similar concept that he calls "sharpening the saw." Sharpening the saw requires renewal, which means to make new (sharpen) again. Renewal is the essence of change. Renewal is simply possessing and producing the courage to participate in a transformational process. Covey relates sharpening the saw to the four most critical areas of our being that continually experience change. The four areas are physical, social/emotional, spiritual, and mental state of being. For Covey, every aspect of our being must experience ongoing change in order to experience happiness and fulfillment effectively and successfully. Social renewal looks like new, loving and understanding friendships with people who act and communicate on your level of morality, fun and creativity. What about improved emotions? How would you feel with less anger, stress, negativity, or even more joy, peace, and compassion? Imagine a new spirituality. Envision renewed harmony with self, God, and others. Imagin new peace and serenity about the affairs of your life and world around you. What a gift that can be to your current state of confidence, self-esteem, and motivation. How would you feel to lose twenty pounds or gain twenty pounds of lean muscle mass? Could you get into a smaller evening gown or finally take that beach vacation? Would the change give you more energy for family outings, community involvement, and extracurricular activity?

It is critical to survive and thrive in change rather than wither up and die. It's easy to quit. What's difficult but rewarding is weathering the change around you and in you until you emerge greater. Emergence means to move away from something and come into view. In many cases, we don't "come into view" until we have survived enough development to properly steward greatness, prosperity, destiny, influence, or power. You must emerge. It's essential to set and emergence goal. An emergence goal happens when you possess a mental picture of your ideal future and plaster it on the canvas of your mind every day until you become it. Until you physically touch it. Until you walk in it. Until you cannot be deny it. The steps for emergence for one person may be more difficult than the steps of another. Nevertheless, keeping rhythm will put you in the gym of endurance building so that you come into view looking great. Emergence requires adjustments.

Small adjustments of attitude can bring out your inner beauty or wisdom. A change in diet or meal plan can create a loss of a few pounds a week and reflect your awesome waistline or physique. A change in countenance, maybe an occasional smile, may become the new habit that attracts your "knight in shining armor" or the lady of your dreams. A slight change in self-development can send you into a much-needed career trajectory rewarding you with a new position, raise, or financial path. Modifying your schedule, turning off the television and giving more time to your goals could result in authoring your book, meeting work deadlines, impressing your boss, or launching that new business idea.

Peel yourself out of the nostalgia of the infamous "comfort zone" and launch out into the adventurous path of the unknown. Who knows what awaits you. Maybe you will like it after all. Maybe this is the exact point and time in your life when you should be reading this book and planning your most significant and brilliant growth strategy! Sharpen the saw! As Jim Rohn once said in his book Twelve Pillars, "What you become directly influences what you get."

Meaningful Over Menial

Please don't all into the temptation of majoring on the minors. Society has adopted this saying because it's universal. Many people fail to prioritize effectively from day-to-day. This is another critical area of growing into greatness. Major on meaningful and not menial. I am not suggesting that small things or that baby steps are not important – they are. However, you must focus on the little things and baby steps that produce the most benefit toward who you believe that you are. This step requires great discipline. Discipline alone can produce rapid results in the direction of your goals and dreams. *It's important to discipline yourself out of menial things before meaningful things.* Refuse to spend time, energy, and life, which are our most profitable human assets, on low value tasks. Low value tasks are tasks that deliver very little gain or success to the achievement of your goals and dreams. Left to ourselves, we lose sight of the bigger picture. What can you possibly be losing sight of that is hurting your growth and potential?

Discipline is necessary to keep cohesion, continuity, and collaboration between what you believe and where you are going. Your dreams, family, and goals deserve order. Order can be the most difficult habit to develop. Order requires constant and consistent work, effort, and energy. It means knowing how to practice delayed gratification-something our society, as of late, has been trained to avoid. Order requires telling yourself no – a lot! Discipline requires developing a high enough threshold for pain so that you achieve results. Hebrews 12:11 teaches that, "For a moment, all discipline seems painful rather than pleasant, but later it yields the peaceful fruit of righteousness to those who have been trained by it." (NKJV) Discipline is trains the body to build constraint. What we need more of is restraint. Without restraint failure is eminent. The Apostle Paul speaking of his intense life of restraint wrote in 1 Corinthians 9:27, "I discipline my body and keep it under control, lest after preaching to others, I myself should be disqualified." (ESV)

Order requires focus, intense focus on your purpose, goals, and dreams. Dave Ramsey, author of the book *Financial Peace*, says that you must learn to "live like no one else so that you can live like no one else." I'm sure that you've heard this before. However, the necessary habits to live like no one else in order to live like no one else require order. Believe me. I have tried it and failed many times until I finally chose my greatness over my gratification. Can your life use a little more order? Imagine if your home-life, work-life, and community-life were all in order. How much time would you save completing tasks? How much easier would it be to plan for a vacation or purchase that dream home? Start creating the order you need today by making a few adjustments and changes consistently over time and watch the compound effect of your actions. Learn to love discipline.

Discipline Requires a System

Brain Tracy, Success Mentor and Author wrote, "Success is not an accident. Failure is not an accident, either. What happens to you is not by luck or coincidence. It is the result of unchanging law." The Aristotelian Principle of Causality, originated by the Western Philosopher Aristotle, helps us to relate to life built around systems. There are more systems at work and at play around us than we often give credit. All of life is a system. For instance, consider the Law of Cause and Effect for it helps bring light to the systems around us. *The Law of Cause and Effect is considered a physics concept and centers around the whole idea of universal energy. It basically suggests that for every action or force there is an equal or greater reaction or force.* So, there is a delicate balance of causes and effects that are taking place around us apart from our acceptance or acknowledgement of them. Nature and life are balanced on a system of cause and effect. For example, if you wanted to add another ten pounds of muscle to your already nicely chiseled physique, you would need to engage the Law of Cause and Effect.

You would add protein to your diet, additional cardio or weightlifting to your exercise plan, and cut out fatty food, as well as some carbohydrates. Your change of habits as mentioned above would be the "cause." If repeated consistently on a workout regimen, these changed habits will result in an additional ten pounds of muscle mass; thus, the results would be the "effect." All of life responds to a system. It is virtually impossible for you to practice this workout regimen consistently and remain at the same level of muscle mass or weight. Therefore, the change that your body experiences validates that the system works.

When you increase your learning, you systematically increase your knowledge. As you increase your knowledge, you achieve more, derive at more success, gain promotions, and ultimately develop greater wisdom and opportunity. The change is proof that the system works. In contrast, a negative and destructive cause or energy will have a negative effect. If you do not exercise regularly and practice proper eating, you will ultimately lose muscle mass and gain fat. The change is proof that the system works. Both healthy and unhealthy systems respond in accordance with the universal Law of Cause and Effect. Change validates that systems are working. There are changes taking place all around you on a daily basis. Learning to embrace change quickly better equips you to have the right response to the systems at work in your life. Refuse to run from change! Simply chalk it up as a working system in your life. Take control of your emotions and responses to the system and gain the most benefit from it. After all, you have dreams and goals to achieve!

You Reap What You Sow

The idea that changes validate systems is a biblical concept as well. Consider how the Law of Cause and Effect is in operation within the Law of Sowing and Reaping. The Law of Sowing and Reaping, as taught in the Bible by Jesus, points out that there is a system to acquire blessings, favor, and whole life balance.

The Law of Sowing and Reaping is often referred to as "Seedtime and Harvest" in many religious denominations. The law, as stated by Jesus in the book of Luke, one of the New Testament books of the Bible, says *"Give, and it will be given to you. They will pour into your lap a good measure— pressed down, shaken together, and running over [with no space left for more]. For with the standard of measurement you use [when you do good to others], it will be measured to you in return."* (Amplified Bible)

Plainly put, as you give (cause or seed) you receive (effect or harvest). In addition, the method and measure in which you give (cause) will be the method and measure in which you receive (effect). This is one of the universal systems at work in your life in which you either recognize and acknowledge or fail to recognize and acknowledge. Either way, the system works based on the Law of Cause and Effect or in this case The Law of Sowing and Reaping. In addition, the Law of Sowing and Reaping yields fruit of divine change far beyond material and financial circumstance.

Learning from the Bible's historical presence and theological impact abroad, the New Testament book of Galatians also provides insight into the divine systems at work. The Apostle Paul, author of the Galatian letter, writes to his audience at Galatia and abroad a message indicating how much of life's circumstances or benefits correlate to sowing and reaping. Galatians 6:7(AMP) says, *"Do not be deceived, God is not mocked [He will not allow Himself to be ridiculed, nor treated with contempt nor allow His precepts to be scornfully set aside]; for whatever a man sows, this and this only is what he will reap. For the one who sows to his flesh [his sinful capacity, his worldliness, his disgraceful impulses] will reap from the flesh ruin and destruction, but the one who sows to the Spirit will from the Spirit reap eternal life. Let us not grow weary or become discouraged in doing good for at the proper time we will reap, if we do not give in."*

Systems Check

Most modern vehicles come equipped with a check engine light. The function of the check engine light, typically located somewhere on the dashboard, is to report on how certain systems of the vehicle are operating. If you're low on oil or transmission fluid or if the car is running hot, the check engine light will alarm you by changing colors or posting some type of icon. When the engine is functioning as it should, the check engine light never comes on. The engine's computer remains in tune with the rhythm and systems of the car. This leads me to a few critical questions to consider. How are you adapting to the reality of the sowing and reaping principle that is at work around you? How do you know when you are off track? Are you paying attention to whatever signals of growth you need? What's malfunctioning? Better yet, do you care even about being broken, stagnate, or out of rhythm? Change validates that systems are working and functioning properly. The changes in your anatomy, psychology, and physiology express that the system within you is working. Changes in nature, business, technology, and economy all reflect the success or failure of working systems. Your home life needs the support of proven social and relationship systems. Do you have them? Are they working? What changes should you embrace to support those proven systems such as communication, honesty, love, forgiveness, and support? Your company or business requires the support of systems. How well are you at identifying, adapting, adopting, and flourishing within those systems? What deviations do you need to make to be in the right rhythm of change? How can you benefit from the interpersonal systems of your church, circle of influence, and community? Look for signs of systems all around you and how they are working. Seek out how you are influencing or resisting working systems. Especially divine systems of seedtime and harvest. Be relentless and you will succeed in the systems around you and within your public and private world.

MQ "Maturity Quotient"

What's your MQ? How do you know? Are you immature, moderately mature, or considerably mature? Not just maturity as in responsibility, although that is critical also, but maturity as in growing into a version of your best self. Joshua Liebman, Author, and Clergyman said, *"Maturity is achieved when a person postpones immediate pleasures for long-term values."* Maturity comes from a Latin word that means ripeness. Have you ever experimented with observing the maturity process for a person or plant and observed how much the person or plant changed? Maturity is all about the endgame. Capitulating to "endgame" suffering exponentially increase success outcomes. As living organisms mature, they change. This is also transferrable to people groups, society, systems, business, etc. Anything with life-force and energy matures. As it matures, it may take on different forms, shapes, and personalities. Thus, validating that maturity is an outgrowth of change. The reshaping occurs through a growth or development process. Change will mature you through the metamorphosis of reshaping. A ripe apple doesn't start out in its' final form. It begins as a seed in the ground. The seed then cross-pollinates with other seeds. Next, it germinates deep beneath the dark, damp dirt. After germination it breaks forth from the dirt as a budding plant. Someone along the growth process develops branches then fruit on the branches. Finally, the apples mature into a ripened state. The process generally takes about 8-10 years. The apple seed has to submit to the "endgame" strategy if it wants to develop, mature, ripen and live its' destiny and greatness. Again, the endgame is a long game. It means postponing immediate pleasure as stated by Joshua Liebman.

Initiating change reveals that you are or have matured. Many may never reach this point. Many may fully ripen. It's one thing to adapt to change. But it's an entirely different ball game when you are courageous enough to initiate it. Maturity is one of the most impressive signs of your growth process. It screams and yells, "Now there's a mature person!" Consider the captivation process of how a seed evolves, germinates, buds, and then blooms into a full-blown fruit, vegetable, or plant. It reflects the dynamic of human change. Each stage of the plant growth process gives it a unique, sometimes small, change or adjustment in form, color, and maturity.

Change does the same for us. As we experience change, especially self-initiated change, we explore new worlds of how we think, act, and feel. Thus, the internal change is expressed in our external form.

Seek to Ripen

I remember watching my youngest son grow into a muscular, athletic young man. As a child, he was "chubby." His cheeks hung low like plums or peaches on a tree. His little round face was like a perfectly baked cookie or pie. He had a head full of curly hair. His legs were "chubby." I wish I could show you a picture. He was the cutest little guy. He was so "chubby" that some found it a little bit of a challenge to pick him up and lift him to the air in their arms. Except me, of course. I was such a proud daddy. So much so that for his first three years, I took him everywhere with me except work. Board meetings-he was my partner. Weight room-he tagged along. Grocery store-there! Hanging with the "fellas"-you better believe it-sidekick! So, I was very comfortable holding my "chubby" son. Because he was so "chubby," many of my friends, family, and associates assumed he would ultimately stay that way. We knew the reality of baby-fat and took that into consideration, but he was so plump that we figured he would hold on too much of it.

Boy where we wrong! By the time he was five years old, he was the perfect picture of a slim, energetic, toned child. As I have watched his body change and mature over the years, I never imagined that he would develop to be so chiseled. Not to mention, the facial hair and deep tone of voice. Yet, as his mind and his body changed, they both matured. He is now taller than me, over six feet tall. He was a D1 athlete and played college football on a scholarship as the top wide receiver in the nation. Now, literally has muscles popping out all over his body and I really feel like a little shrimp when he comes around. Funny? I know. My point is that with his change came his maturity. He ripened! Though he surely has more stages and phases of ripening to experience, I think that you get my point.

Your financial wisdom, your physical health, your relationship skills, your dating skills, your ability to hope and dream, your psychology, your ambitions, your marriage, your optimism, your self-esteem, and your life will mature when you change. Remember, you reap externally what you sow internally. You are able to meet the "ripened" qualifications for every area of your life if and when you change. What does it feel like to know exactly what to do and maybe even when to do it? How would your life differ if you managed money well, practiced healthy eating habits, blossomed in relationships, succeeded at dreams and goals, developed balanced emotions and a healthy, positive thought life? Would you feel and show more maturity? Would you say that you were ripening? How does the idea of being ripe transfer into everything in which you are currently invested? Every relationship, business deal, career move, and destiny shift require a ripened you. Can you do it? Will you change to get there? I know you will because you are relentless! Not only are you relentless, but you are also intelligent!

Intelligent People Change

Bruce Barton, Author, and Politician made a statement that I find so appropriate for this section. I'm not sure of the quotes' origin but he says, *"When you are through changing, you are through."* I simply love this nugget of wisdom. It's relevant. It's timeless. And it's profound. If change is inevitable, and it is, you must apply a reasonable measure of intelligence and partner that level of intelligence with change in order to grow into greatness. In fact, this cannot be a one-time application. It cannot be a feel-good application. It has to become a life journey application. Changing with the rhythm of YOUR times and seasons of life is evidence of intelligence. The act suggests that you have allowed your brain to express its reasoning ability to keep you functioning within the realities of your inner/outer world. Here's is some sobering news, if you fail to progress in any area that demands or requires change, then you are demonstrating a low level of intelligence. You are saying, "Brain, I don't want you to work right now. Don't do your job!"

What is intelligence? There are several definitions for intelligence. A simple definition is your ability to learn, reason, and understand. Now you do not need a PhD to learn, reason, and understand. You were born with the gift of intelligence. Intelligence is the partner of change because intelligent people understand the need and benefits of change. Where there is intelligence, there is change. Viewing intelligence from a broad perspective you will find that there are many types of intelligence. The history of psychological study proves the existence of many intelligences such as naturalist intelligence (people who are nature smart), musical intelligence (people who are music smart), linguistic intelligence (people who are word smart), interpersonal intelligence (people who are people smart), and spatial intelligence (people who are picture smart).

This is not an exhaustive list but gives you an idea of the extent of intelligence. You probably fall into one or more of these categories proving that you are intelligent. Do not assume that you are not intelligent based on the dominant ideas or types of intelligent people in your life or circumstances. Your intelligence just may be different from others. You should feel good about your type of intelligence. You were created with it, born with it. Your type of intelligence, if honored and valued, will take you far in life. It will help you adapt to change in order to promote your growth and maturity. Soon you will see your full potential blossom by your intelligence type. As a matter of fact, according to an article in Psychology Today, written by Dr. Ronald Riggio, Professor of Leadership and Psychology, the three types of intelligence needed for success today are academic (known as verbal), emotional (recognizing and managing emotion) and social (relational and interpersonal) intelligence. The benefit of this discovery is that each of these types of intelligence can be developed, groomed, and learned by anyone with any of the other types of intelligence. Remember, intelligence is the ability to learn, reason, and understand.

Academic or verbal intelligence is measured in a unit called IQ.

Emotional Intelligence is measured in a unit called EQ. Social Intelligence is measured in a unit called SQ. Since we just have to give a measurement or title to most things let me introduce the CQ.

CQ is how we should measure how intelligently we respond to change. CQ stands for our level of "change intelligence." After all, as Bruce Barton said, "When you are through changing, you are through."

The Right Attitude Fuels Growth

Change is the partner of intelligence. Brian Tracy, in his book, *Change Your Thinking, Change Your Life* (MJF Books, 2003), writes that there are two major factors that stand in the way of you using more of your natural intelligence. They are psychosclerosis and homeostasis. Big words right! Fret not, I will simplify them for you. The first big word, psychosclerosis, is to have a hardened attitude. The second big word, homeostasis, is to seek to always do or say what you have always done or said in the past. Both states of mind can cause you to fail at applying the necessary level of intelligence to produce change. I have encountered countless people during my lifetime who have a hard attitude or are in love with repeating what they have already done. T.D. Jakes, in his book, Reposition Yourself, wrote *"The sad memories of a lost opportunity have made many people bitter the rest of their lives. Often it is not the fatigue of the Olympic competitor that is debilitating as much as it is the feeling that if he had lunged farther, or pushed harder, he might have been holding the golden cup of victory as opposed to the bottled water of defeat."*

People with hard attitudes or who love repeating the same old system or approach to life are stuck and hardly ever change. They live life stuck in the past, hurt by old circumstances, living a life of fear and unforgiveness. They are powerlessly trapped in a world of insecurity, tradition, and opinion instead of thriving in a world of confidence, change, and truth. My heart goes out to people in these conditions. They have little faith. They refuse to take risks, big or small. They accept whatever life feeds or deals with them. Their favorite quote is, "You know that you have to play the cards that life deals you." Why not just get up from that card table and create a new card game altogether? Mary Kay Ash, a self-made billionaire, changed the landscape of network marketing. She has built a successful cosmetic business known as Mary Kay.

She said, *"There are three types of people in this world: those who make things happen, those who watch things happen and those who wonder what happened."* She may not have originated the quote, but her success and innovation qualify her to postulate it. When you refuse to add intelligence to change or to change intelligently, you will ultimately be the person who "wondered what happened." To avoid this entrapment become relentless about greatness and grow into it. Refuse to get stuck on the past and how things "used to be." Embrace change in whatever form it takes. Flow with the rhythm of change. Initiate the change necessary to achieve your goals. As a matter of fact, be a game-changer. How, may you ask? Infuse change into life, work, and your surroundings. Be innovative and creative. Most of all be intelligent enough to see change coming and get in the momentum or set the pace. Now that is using your intelligence.

The Beauty and Creativity of Change

There is an inherent measure of beauty in the creativity of change. When someone or something comes into full blossom, destiny, or greatness, it communicates that awesomeness of God. It helps the world explore the beauty of imagination. Louis Schwartzberg, American director, producer, and cinematographer once said, *"Metamorphosis has always been the greatest symbol of change for poets and artists. Imagine that you could be a caterpillar one moment and a butterfly the next."* A phenomenal expression of change is the butterfly. Louis Schwartzberg has been able to artistically beautify the connection between the animals of nature and compare them with people and the planet. In his own words, you my dear friend can be a caterpillar one moment and a butterfly the next. Did you catch that? Did it register with you? Let's try it this way. Small acts of metamorphosis over time may introduce you to life as a caterpillar but later introduce you to the world as a butterfly. Your next resilient act of change can be the very thing that catapults your career, income, status, influence, impact, personality, marriage, etc. to 'butterfly status' which in the butterfly's case is its destiny.

Much of the Grow Into Your Greatness 21 Key Principles to Transform and Access Your Destiny is formulated and written from the concept of the butterfly's metamorphosis. Its natural, beautiful, internal, and external evolution is the epitome of becoming on the outside, the change that you make on the inside. The butterfly grows into greatness. *From crawling on a slab of steaming hot concrete in the scorching summer's sun as a caterpillar to flying high above the rooftops in the coolness of a blowing breeze with a multi-color coat, the butterfly accesses destiny through change.*

It is simply amazing, and it is about to happen to you if it has not already happened! First, know this, you are creative, and you are beautiful. In your unique design and being, you are divinely beautiful. You are creative and beautiful. Psalm 139:13-14(ESV) speaks of human beauty, *"For you formed my inward parts; you knitted me together in my mother's womb. I praise you, for I am fearfully and wonderfully made."* Please do not allow life, circumstance, past experiences, self-limiting beliefs, socio-economic status, or anything else to communicate otherwise and accept it. You are creative and beautiful. Take a moment and say that to yourself three times. Say, "I am creative and beautiful." "I am creative and beautiful." "I am creative and beautiful." How does that feel? It should feel great, even awesome, because you are great and awesome!

We experience metamorphosis at all stages of life and states of being like the butterfly. We experience it professionally, spiritually, socially, emotionally, physically, and psychologically. We experience it from adolescence to pre-teen to teenager. We experience it throughout our biological timeline as we grow from infant to adult. Furthermore, we morph more than we know. Sometimes we voluntarily morph. Other times we involuntarily morph. The word morph means to "change completely" which is what the caterpillar does to become a butterfly. After reading this book, you are going to change completely. There is a person in you that has yet to emerge.

There is a new creative you down on the inside of you that needs you to make whatever changes necessary to soar to new heights, expand vision, and experience destiny.

The theatre of your life is now set. The stage is dressed for your next big scene. Your storyline presents you before the audience as a masterful artist painting the Picasso of a lifetime. The crowd is the world, and the world is energetically, passionately, and intensely waiting for the appearance of the new you! Sitting on the edge of their seats are all the people in life that you will touch, inspire, encourage, and serve. They are ahead in the near as well as distant future praying, anticipating, and expecting someone like you to step into their lives and leave them breathless. You are a star. The star of an amazing show. Many have seen you crawl slowly like the caterpillar, inch by inch to small measures of change, success, and destiny. Now is the time to go into your cocoon of change. Now is the opportunity to wall yourself into the process of change. It's time to allow the process to develop your wings and make you as beautiful, amazing, and talented as the butterfly that you truly are. Are you ready? Can you change for destiny? Are you willing to achieve something greater, be greater, and live greater? Greatness is calling you. Will you answer?

Chapter Conclusions

1. List at least ten specific changes that you know, feel, and think that you need to make in order to be happier, achieve more success, fulfill a life-long goal, etc.
2. Take the list of at least ten specific changes and narrow them down to your top three significant changes.
3. Ask someone within your circles of friends, family, co-workers etc. to review your list to confirm the need for these changes. Confirmation provides reinforcement for truth and focus.
4. Out of the three most significant changes choose the one change that you would like to make in the next thirty days. If thirty days is not enough time, narrow the change goals down to small steps and push yourself to achieve as many of the small steps as possible toward the goal in the next thirty days.
5. Get angry with yourself and "GO TO WAR!" Anger is a motivator. Until you get angry about your present condition you will never fight effectively for change. Go to war at achieving your "Change Goal." Remember, be relentless. Be unmerciful on yourself. Take no prisoners.
6. Take a moment and say three times to yourself that you are creative and beautiful. Say, "I am creative and beautiful." "I am creative and beautiful." "I am creative and beautiful." How does that feel?
7. People with hard attitudes or who love repeating the same old system or approach to life are stuck and hardly ever change.

To become someone that you have never been before, you must do something that you have never done before. - Brian Tracy

If nothing ever changed, there'd be no butterflies. - Author Unknown

Chapter 2

The Greater Principle

The Greater Principle suggests that change is most conceivable when it is connected to a greater person or purpose.

Most people hate change. It is a tough saying but there are times when you have to learn to love what you once hated for the greater advancements of your life, career, and well-being. *Associate change to the greatness and success of your life, friendships, goals, and dreams and change will become invaluable and attainable.* The more fluent you are at associating, thinking, and processing change this way, the quicker you will master the skills and focus needed for healthy change. The changes in life are often connected to a greater person or purpose in life. We all have people in our lives that we mentally regard as higher than ourselves. We esteem them through love, affection, and servitude. For many years, it has been my wife and children. There were times when it was my spiritual leader or authority. However, it is always God. This may not be the same for everyone. We all have different reasons why we esteem someone greater or more important than ourselves. These people are in our lives to bring out the best in us. We cherish their opinions, thoughts, actions, and love toward us. They are often the reason we live or at least the reason we strive to succeed at one thing or another. Often, we succeed because of them or the way we feel about them. The Greater Principle is spiritual in essence and profoundly biblical. Philippians 2:3(ESV) teaches, *"Do nothing from selfish ambition or conceit, but in humility count others more significant than yourselves."*

Who might these people be for you? Identifying those in your life in which you esteem higher and more important than you can be the motivation and accountability for change. You should live life and change for those that you care about deeply and the most. Who are they? Are they important enough for you to connect change? Can you credit the reason that you should or can change to the impact or effect that the change will have on them? Maybe the necessary change will provide a better way of life such as more financial stability. Maybe changing a health condition or preventing one through more self-discipline will secure a lifetime of memories for your children or spouse. People in our society make poor choices daily in their eating and exercise routines which is increasing the mortality rate. Children are left to care for parents facing multiple medical issues due to self-inflicted sickness. In many cases these sicknesses could have possibly been prevented by simply connecting change to a greater person.

You do not want to die early and leave your spouse, children, or relatives without the joy of your presence. They are a valuable reason to change. Are they not more important than continuing the destructive eating patterns? Are they more important than the overconsumption of fried foods, fatty foods, sugary foods, salty foods, and unhealthy processed products? Are they not more important than the temporary, momentary ecstasy? If so, change for them! However, esteeming others before you require humility. Achieving greatness first requires that we humble ourselves. Humility is the birthplace of greatness. Humility doesn't necessarily come naturally. Neither is it easy to acquire. If it were easy to acquire, the world would have fewer narcissist, tyrannical leaders, divisive cultures, racism, and the like. When humility doesn't come easy, then spiritual growth is the next best path to get there. Colossians 3:11-13 says, *"So, as those who have been chosen of god, holy and beloved, put on a heart of compassion, kindness, humility, gentleness and patience; bearing with one another, and forgiving each other, whoever has a complaint against anyone; just as the Lord forgave you, so must you do also."* (NASB)

Great Purpose Requires Great Change

Heart traits like compassion, kindness, humility, gentleness, patience, and forgiveness reflect a type of transcendent maturity. Have you ever met someone with these heart traits? Being in their presence is almost like being in the presence of an angel. Change for a greater purpose! Sometimes our purpose for achieving a goal, dream, or change is not big enough. It is not audacious enough. It is not weighty enough. Yet, all around us are people who have learned to connect change, big or small, to the greater causes and missions of humankind. Have you? Think about it. What if making the much needed and necessary changes in your life to better equip the world to manage terrorism? What if it leads to a calculated strategy for world hunger? What if it simply eases the burden of homelessness for the little bag lady up the road?

Sometimes we have to branch outside of the circle of small thinking in order to see the bigger pictures and greater causes in life, community, company, or country. Sometimes it is our low self-esteem or faulty internal story that says, "I'm not important enough to make a big difference." That type of thinking is what I call "stinking thinking" and is as far from the truth as it can be. What if Dr. Martin Luther King thought the same way? What if Bill Gates thought his computer ideas would not make a difference? What if Mark Zuckerberg gave up on Facebook? Or Jeff Bezos listened to his former boss and walked away from his ideas about Amazon? You are important. You can make a dent in the universe or at least a scratch in your family and community. Some people are "denters'", and some are "scratchers."

By the way, here is a little instruction from the Little Instruction Book. *"Don't say you don't have enough time. You have exactly the same number of hours per day that were given to Helen Keller, Pasteur, Michelangelo, Mother Teresa, Leonardo da Vinci, Thomas Jefferson, and Albert Einstein."* –Life's Little Instruction Book

Here is a secret. When others benefit from your change, so do you. The greater person is within you-the future you. The greater purpose is yours to possess. It is your greatest life purpose. Change is not a waste of time, effort, and energy. Good or challenging, it is valuable. Remember, change either brings new lessons or new life. Life begins with change. Life ends with change. Consider the butterfly as an example of how change is connected to a greater purpose or person. For much of our journey, we will look closely at what the butterfly experiences. It is a simple approach with profound lessons that you can master for the many changes that you will experience in life.

CHANGE FOR YOUR DESTINY!

The search for destiny is a part of the human quest. Everyone old enough to feel the sense of meaning burning in their hearts has grappled with the question, "Why am I here?" Organic change is how purpose develops without any creative manipulation or desperate plights to God. It happens through the process of metamorphism. Metamorphosis is a big word for change. It means complete change to be exact. It is where we get the whole idea of being transformed. I have never witnessed a greater metamorphosis like that of a butterfly. The difference between the beginning state and the final state is memorizing, beautiful, and mind-blowing. If there was ever a creature, in my opinion, whose total change displays greatness it is the butterfly. Other than the human body, the butterfly's transformational process is second to none.

The butterfly changes for destiny. And it is organic. Please don't misinterpret my statement. Without question, the butterfly has to "grind," put in work, and flow with the rhythm of change. However, when it yields to the process, parts of it are effortless. If you cannot fathom nor find any other reason on the planet, in your heart, or in your family to change, change for the sake of your destiny. It is the reason that you are alive and on this planet. The most discouraging life to lead is one without pursuit of destiny. It is a life without aim, focus, or destination. Yet so many people opt out. It is often said that the richest soil in the world is not the gold mines or oil fields but the cemeteries. Why is that so? In them lie the unseen destinies and dreams of people who opted out.

The butterfly goes through four major stages of change. First the egg stage then the larva, next the pupa stage and finally the adult stage. We will exam them all and compare them with how we mentally and behaviorally process through our own stages of change. Maybe if you know where you are in the process, you can assist along the way. At each stage, there is a greater purpose than just going through the process. The butterfly is changing for destiny. So, will you! Destiny holds the key to its amazing beauty. This holds true for you also!

Change is and always will be a process. Fear not. Process is exactly how God forms us. It is His way of maturing and developing us as vessels of honor and glory. It is indicative of growing into greatness. When God prepares to create or do something new, He cloaks it in process. In Mark 4, Jesus using a parable about farming to illustrate the coming of God's Kingdom on earth say, "The earth produces the crops on its own. First a leaf blade pushes through, then the heads of wheat are formed, and finally the grain ripens." (NLT). This parable demonstrates the reality that change is always a process. The seed metamorphosis process is directly responsible for its' harvest and destiny. Destiny is ripened grain worthy to be consumed by creation. We have to learn to be patient in the process. Mastering patience is always a process until we are purged of all earthly desires and want nothing more than to please God and be who He has sent us here to be.

The study of psychology suggests that human behavior happens in stages and phases. We do not just up and change. Change takes time. It requires patience with yourself as well as others. We change through a five-stage process and some even believe six. These five or six stages help us understand where we are in the change process and how to successfully embody the goal. In the realm of psychology, the stages are labeled pre-contemplation, contemplation, preparation, action, and maintenance. The sixth is often called relapse. However, we are already optimistic and decreeing favor over your process that you will not perpetually relapse! Remember, however, that change begins in our minds.

Destiny and purpose are the most rewarding stages of life. Achieving them will require change. Constant change can be volatile and challenging to say the least. How can you lay hold of that which often seems evasive and hidden from the naked eye? Destiny and purpose are often exposed the life's stages. Yet, what often appears is the trait, skill, or concept in which you need mastery in order to get to the next stage of change, destiny, purpose, or success. Remember, achieving the ultimate level of purpose, destiny, or success is not about the end goal. Instead, it is about the person that you become by the process, like the butterfly. Destiny is not a trophy at the end of life's pursuit for identity or the reason for life. Destiny is the state of being that you master along the way until we see the final picture. It is from this understanding that your mindset begins to influence your emotions toward change.

Here is the model mindset, "Relate change to someone and something greater than yourself." In everything that you initiate and endure in life quote this to yourself, "The change that I'm experiencing is connected to someone or something greater than myself." Furthermore, this mindset will give you the exhilaration and enthusiasm necessary to initiate change that requires longsuffering and delayed gratification.

A female butterfly has to lay an egg called an ovum on a food plant to start the growth process. The egg cannot get there on its own. It is connected to a greater person. Changing or defining a rhythm of change often requires someone or something ushering you into action. There are greater people all around you and placed in your path to morph you into the beautiful and creative butterfly you are designed to reflect. We change more by the conditions that we are "laid in" than the conditions that we create for ourselves.

Do What You Have Never, Ever Done

Eleanor Roosevelt, Former First Lady of United States said, *"You must do the thing you think you cannot do."* Surely, we can think of a necessary change in our life that needs addressing. We have been down this fox hole before. We have read all the books on the subject, signed up for the course, and mapped out the strategy. We have even enlisted the help of a friend. The question is, "Why don't we succeed?" I am not suggesting that we always fail. I am simply prodding on the question, 'Why don't we succeed?" Take for example some of the general statistics that float around during the time of New Year's resolutions. Did you know that roughly 98% of people who set resolutions fail at them? As a matter of fact, those "experts" of human behavior are now suggesting that we refrain from making them all together. The new trend is to be like the Nike slogan and just do it! Achievement demands mastering the art of putting "your money where your mouth is." The reality is that only a small percentage of people in the world actually determine to see a personal goal through to completion regardless of the intensity level. So, if you are in the 98% who start and stop then repeat the cycle, then ask yourself, why? Was it fear? Was it a lack of focus? Was it too painful? Was there too much rejection or too little support? Only you know. Nevertheless, I have a resolution. *"YOU MUST DO THAT THING THAT YOU THINK YOU CANNOT DO!"* Maybe what you did not do or have not done is stay the course. Maybe you bailed out too soon. Maybe your emotions clouded your vision or passion and you quit. Maybe you just need to apply yourself more.

Wherever the adult butterfly lays the egg, which is normally a food plant of some sort, the egg eats all the nutrients. The egg has to find food supply and nutrients for growth where it has been placed. This may sound a little poetic and even metaphorical, but God is likened unto the female butterfly, and we are the egg needing nurture and change. We seldom get the opportunity to pick each and every condition of life in which we find nurture. However, we can always mentally and psychologically feed off every environment and find healthy growth. Even when growth is learning what not to do. Can you relate to this? Do you always get to choose the course of your life? Do you find that you are "dropped" into situations and circumstances more than getting your choice of where you land? Have you been able to find grace and growth in those situations? I have. Most of life has been this way for me. In each case, I had to do what I have never done in order to be who I have never been.

What can you do to access greatness that you have never, ever done? Try to think completely out of the box. Think outside of your normal life for a moment. Try to focus on ways that you have not. Consider one area in your life that needs change. Now, create a mental list of people to help you that you would not ordinarily approach. Think of at least two resources that excite or challenge you to pursue. Take my advice. Don't be passive. Be aggressive! Scare yourself. Then, scare yourself more by taking a leap of faith to achieve it. I recall challenging one of my mentees to go back to school in his late forties. He was terrified. It was the thing that he had never, ever done. He possessed limiting beliefs that he wasn't smart enough. This narrative destroyed his confidence. Spiraling down this dark rabbit hole of mental torment, he had also concluded that he would not do well working with computers. After some passionate yet hard coaching, I convinced him to do what he had never done. Though terrified, he took the leap of faith. In the end, he passed every course with an A grade. He was pursuing a greater version of himself for destiny. This could be you if you're willing to take the leap!

Can you think of a new approach or method to achieve your goal apart from your normal patterns? Spend some time on this project. Create new feelings about this area of change in your life. In this exercise think courageously. Don't give fear an invitation to the party. Try playing the authority role and in your minds' eye help someone else achieve what you want to achieve. See yourself coaching and training them through the steps and stages. What would you say? How articulate and charismatic would you be? How logical and intuitive is your response? What facts or formulas would you offer?

Finding the nutrients to grow right where you are and feeding them is what prepares you to emerge into the next stage of your awesome life, career, goals, and dreams. Is there a dream that you have yet to fulfill? Do what you have never, ever done to be who you have never, ever been. If all else fails, at least you would have acknowledged the need to change. As Mark Twain, American humorist and writer also pen name for Samuel Langhorne Clemens, once said, *"20 years from now you will be disappointed by the things you didn't do than by the one's you did. So, throw off the bowlines. Sail away from the safe harbor. Catch the trade winds in your sails. Explore. Dream. Discover."*

Chapter Conclusions

1. The Greater Principle suggests that change is most conceivable when it is connected to a greater person or purpose.
2. Take some time to identify the greater person or purpose connected to your most significant area of change. Make a mental or physical list of the person or purpose. Convince yourself of why you esteem the person or purpose higher than yourself.
3. Think of people in your circle of friends, family, and associates who can help you achieve your "change goal." Think outside the box.
4. List all the people that you normally would not approach. List all the resources that you normally would not attempt to acquire.
5. Write out a plan of action that consists of objectives or steps that you have never, ever done.
6. Identify how you can "feed" or gain emotional, physical, psychological, mental, social, and other nutrients where you are, in what you are in. Write down your thoughts.
7. Now, EAT! GROW! Become who you have never been while in the egg stage of changing into the beautiful butterfly that you really are. And if you do not like butterflies-change for destiny.

"Getting over a painful experience is much like crossing monkey bars. You have to let go at some point in order to move forward."

-C.S. Lewis, Author, and Oxford University Professor

"The best thing you can do is the right thing; the next best thing you can do is the wrong thing; the worst thing you can do is nothing."

-Theodore Roosevelt, 26th U. S. President

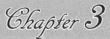

Chapter 3

The Acknowledgment 2Principle

The Acknowledgement Principle suggests that change begins with confessing that a problem exists.

In the previous chapter, The Greater Principle, I concluded with comments on practicing acknowledgement. Nathaniel Branden, in his book Six Pillars of Self Esteem wrote, "I cannot be truly myself, cannot build self-esteem, if I cannot accept myself." (Bantom1994) The Acknowledgement Principle teaches us to admit or confess the need for change that we often ignore. It requires the painstaking process of identifying the problem even when we are the problem. Have you ever had to divulge privately or publicly a weakness or need to change? How long did you dodge the process? How much energy and focus did you invest in covering it up? Count the number of trivial lies you told to hide it? Consider the amounts of money that you spent to mask it? What about all the anger and emotional anguish you experienced to defend it? Was it worth it? Honestly, it's never really worth it. In the moment, it feels worth it but as we mature, we realize being a phony and an imposter is tiring and depressing. We often waste more time, money, energy, etc. in covering up our weaknesses and problems rather than investing in changing them. I have lived this one myself. *We often know our need to change but seldom jump right into action; this is because we are in pre-contemplation mode.*

Practicing Awareness

Whatever you do, refuse to continue to ignore awareness. Awareness has become very popular amongst leadership scholars. As a matter a fact it has permeated corporate America as one of the three parts of emotional intelligence. Emotional intelligence has become a highly sought out competency. The primary three parts are self-awareness, self-management, and relational equity. Awareness begins once we have internalized and even recognized the need for change but have neither acknowledged it nor plan to act on it anytime soon. Sound familiar? I am sure it does. Maybe you are in this state of mind in an area of your life. I will tell you now, you will never change until you acknowledge what exists. Psychologists call this the pre-contemplation mode of behavioral change. Behavior has to be acknowledged before it is transformed. Wayne Gretzky, The Great One, considered the greatest National Hockey League player of all times, once said, *"You miss 100 percent of the shots you never take."* If you ever wondered what state of mind you were in as you toyed with much needed change, dodged much needed change, or simply brushed off that glaring light shining brightly on that area of most needed change, now you know that you were pre-contemplating. Although it is natural, it can also be the sticking point or point of complacency. Some people never come out of pre-contemplation. It is basically a state of mind whereby you keep swatting away the thoughts of change as if they are fruit flies circling around your watermelon.

When you fail to shift from pre-contemplation, it becomes a devastating habit. It is devastating to your goals, dreams, career, and destiny. It keeps you from your ultimate potential and from succeeding at change. Warren Buffet, Philanthropist, and self-made billionaire said, *"In a chronically leaking boat, energy devoted to changing vessels is more productive than energy devoted to patching leaks."* Most people who dwell here often look back over their life at the end and say what could have, would have, and should have happened. Destiny is achievable when you shift out of pre-contemplation mode.

The words of Nathaniel Branden were true at the time he wrote them and remain true today. Branden said, *"I cannot overcome a fear whose reality I deny. I cannot correct a problem in the way I deal with my associates if I will not admit it exists. I cannot change traits I insist I do not have. I cannot forgive myself for an action I will not acknowledge having taken."* Ask yourself the question, "Am I ignoring what I need to change?" There is a saying that ignorance is bliss. According to the Cambridge Idioms Dictionary, this means that what you don't know won't hurt you. Another opinion is it is better not to know than to know. You can pick whichever you like but the conclusion of the matter regarding ignorance is that ignorance costs. The one who is ignorant pays with wasted time, energy, knowledge, opportunity, etc. I would dare to say that what you are ignorant about hurts. For example, if you lived in Texas for ten years on a ten-acre farm that you owned, then relocated ten miles up the road, and ten months later heard that someone else discovered oil on that land you once owned, would your ignorance be costly? I would think so.

Are you choosing to ignore an area of change in your life? Could this act be costing you years off of your lifeline, happiness in your home, friendships with constituents, peace of mind, career progress, or even financial opportunity? Are you treating an area of change like it is a fruit fly- small, barely visible, and easy to crush at the slight of thought? For a long time, I ignored getting therapy for the brokenness and abuse that I experienced as a child and teenager. When I look back over my life, I can clearly see the price I paid in friendships, family growth, mental clarity, maturity, career development, etc. The evidence is everywhere and so is yours. I have done this while improving my health, managing anger, and stewarding resources. And maybe so have you. The areas and conditions in which you have ignored may not mirror mine, but the reality is that at times we all ignore what we need to change.

Overcoming Denial

Mark Twain once said, "Denial ain't just a river in Egypt." Funny stuff. I laugh every time I read or hear this. Maybe I'm just corny like that. Nevertheless, health psychologists support the idea that your success or failure outcomes can be measured by your ability or inability to change behaviors. Adapting new behaviors that are healthy and productive for your growth areas and goals are key to progress. Please do not defend bad habits as some so eloquently do!

Please do not pretend what is real does not exist! Please do not assume that the inevitable cannot happen to you! Before you can change, you must acknowledge that which you choose to ignore. People often fail to accept any contradictory conclusion about how they see themselves. This can lead to a life of denial and believing that the change taking place before their very eyes is not really happening. Regardless of the number of red flags, indicators, reasons, or cuddly confirmations of the change or the need to change, they deny that the issue is real or the necessity to address it has value. This is called being defensive. When you become defensive, it is because you have become fearful.

Fear causes you to become defensive towards truth. Let me tell you a funny story about denial. There once was a couple living out in the desert plains in a Middle Eastern country. One day three visitors passed by them. The old man seeing the three visitors stopped them as they were passing by and invited them to stay for a drink of water and a bite to eat. They agreed. The old man quickly ran into his tent and with excitement in his weakening voice he requested his wife, the old woman, to prepare bread for the visitors. Afterwards, he rushed into his servant and with the same energy requested that he prepare the best choice of meat.

After the meal was prepared with warmth and tender care, the old man delightfully presented the meal to the visitors and served them with gladness. Soon afterwards, as the old woman looked on from the door entrance, one of the servants made an unusual statement. He said, "A year from this day your wife will have a child." Tickled with amazement and a bit of sarcasm, the old woman, laughed within herself and thought, "How can my husband and I have a child at this old age? This is so funny to me." Immediately, one of the visitors asked the old man, "Why did your wife laugh at my saying?" At this point fear gripped the old woman. She stepped out of the shadows of the tent's entrance and hesitatively said, "Oh, I did not laugh." The visitor, having clearly heard the old woman laugh said, "Yes, you did laugh." Do you find this story interesting or maybe even funny? The characters in this brief story are Abraham and Sarah, two people out of a Bible story in the book of Genesis. Regardless of who they are or where the story is written, the moral is this: fear can move you to deny the truth. The following year, Sarah conceived in her old age and birthed a son by the name of Isaac.

Practice Honesty

Are you fearful toward an area or habit that you know needs to change? Maybe it is an area that you are growing more aware of each day and are fearful of addressing. Did you know that fear has been identified as the top obstacle in adult success? Is that you? Are you living your adult life in fear of changing or even denying that change around you? Denial syndrome also called alternative belief is a phase that therapists say those overcoming addictions often entertain. Lingering here will keep you trapped in a cycle of failure and loss of traction in achieving your goals and dreams. The only solution to denial is transparency and acknowledgement; some would call it plain old honesty. Once you derive at a place in your thinking where you refuse to accept the indicators, red flags, symptoms, and subtle confirmations of where you are stuck, try practicing some gut-wrenching honesty. Here is a task for you. Ask three of the dearest and wisest people in your life (be sure one is a business associate), "Name one growth area in my life that you feel can help me improve." Without bias or recourse of action, simply listen to their feedback with an open mind.

Go into the discussion with a willingness to accept their opinion and observation with gladness. Value their worth and effort in your life as a dear person to you and seek to be open and vulnerable. You will find that this exercise can change your life dramatically and move you closer to greatness. *When you begin educating yourself about where you are and how to move forward, destiny awaits you. Gaining this knowledge will help you change and lead you to the next practical steps in overcoming denial which are confrontation and feedback. This all becomes a process of raising your awareness.* Do not be afraid of the process. As a matter of fact, make it an act of courage. Muster up the boldness to engage what could be an emotional dialogue and conquer any denial in your life. You've got this! Believe in yourself.

Chapter Conclusions

1. The Acknowledgement Principle teaches us to admit or confess the need for change that we often ignore. It requires the painstaking process of identifying the problem even when you are the problem.
2. Ask yourself the question, "Am I ignoring what I need to change?"
3. Behavior has to be acknowledged before it is transformed.
4. When you fail to shift from pre-contemplation, it becomes a devastating habit. It is devastating to your goals, dreams, career, and destiny. It keeps you from your ultimate potential and from succeeding at change.
5. Do not defend bad habits! Do not pretend what is real does not exist! Do not assume that the inevitable cannot happen to you! Be flexible and you will live a full and prosperous life.
6. Ask three of the dearest and wisest people in your life, (be sure one is a business associate), "Name one growth area in my life that you feel can help me improve?" Without bias or recourse of action, simply listen to their feedback with an open mind.
7. When you begin educating yourself about where you are and how to move forward, destiny awaits you. Gaining this knowledge will help you change and lead you to the next practical steps in overcoming denial which are confrontation and feedback.

It is hard to kick against the pricks.
-Holy Bible

The thorn from the bush one has planted, nourished, and pruned, pricks more deeply, and draws more blood.

-Maya Angelou, Poet, and Actress

Chapter 4

The Prick Principle

The Prick Principle suggests that we are often aware of our need to change through what we continually sense within.

Change does not always require external forces or confirmations. We really do not need anyone to repeatedly inform us of what we already know about ourselves. We all have inner convictions. Our inner convictions alone, when acknowledged, regardless of their intrusive nature, are enough to move us to change. We were designed to change whenever necessary regardless of our environment. We are the most unique and intelligent creature on the planet. We are wired to shift, change, and adapt with the times, transitions, advancements, occasions, seasons, etc. Everything we need to inform us is in us. The challenge is paying attention and adding value to what is going off inside. Thus, the idea of the Prick Principle. What does it mean to prick? The word prick means to pierce with a sharp point, to pain, or to puncture. Change often begins with what is also theologically referred to as a pricking process.

Let me first ask you this, "Is there something eating away at you?" Is there something that is just nagging in the back of your mind? Is there something weighing so heavily on your heart that you lose focus when it is on your mind? Do you begin to drift off into space when your awareness is aroused regarding a particular area of life, habit, or condition? If so, that feeling is the "prick" of change luring you into action. You do not have to be a highly intuitive person, meaning significantly in tune with your innermost feelings, to experience pricking. Pricking is subtle but packs a powerful sting because pricking happens in your deepest places- your heart, your mind, and your soul. We can never prepare for change without first experiencing the prick of change.

What is pricking you? An even better question to ask is, "What has pricked you in the past?" The Apostle Paul, one of the Bible writers in the New Testament and highly esteemed church planter, experienced the prick of change before he experienced the preparation of change that truly altered the trajectory of his destiny. Paul, whose name was actually Saul during the first phase of his pricking process, did not begin his adult journey as an Apostle. As a matter of fact, he was quite the opposite. He was a dangerous and judgmental religious leader who opposed religions other than Judaism.

As an act of opposition, he sought to rid the people of Jerusalem and surrounding areas of practicing Christianity. Whether it was an adult or child did not matter to Saul. He violently and relentlessly disposed of them, even to the degree of invading their homes and dragging them through city streets to be imprisoned and stoned to death. Saul was very passionate about his beliefs and their opposition to them. Thinking he was doing God a favor or at least acting out God's will, Paul sought the approval of officials in high places to affirm and even authenticate his actions in the form of legal documents. Upon receiving this approval, Saul launched his campaign to destroy any Christian he could find. He hunted them down. Mercilessly. However, it is historically recorded in the New Testament book of Acts 9:1-6, that one day as Saul traveled on a road to the city of Damascus, he was confronted and even overwhelmed by a marvelous and brilliant light. The brilliance of the light shined so intensely that Saul was thrust from his towering beast of a horse to the ground and lie helpless in the dirt. Out of the shining light came a voice, a voice soon revealed to Saul as Jesus Christ, a voice asking a life-altering question, "Saul why do you persecute me? Don't you find it hard to kick against the pricks?"

From the words of Saul's very own testimony, we can see that while Saul was persecuting and destructively violating Christians, he was experiencing the power of the Lord's conviction inside. The time had come to acknowledge what he had always ignored. Since he would not listen to the constant urge to change deep from within himself, he experienced "other initiated change" which is often more painful than heeding our inner self. Saul was now face-to-face with the reality of the sharp piercing that he had experienced all along. Although acting without any regard or remorse for his misdealing, Saul was struggling with God's conviction.

The prick was preparing him for change that altered his destiny. Another name for prick is goad. A goad was an instrument or weapon, sometimes ten feet long, used by ploughmen to steer or guide oxen. Like the goad, the pricking is an instrument of destiny, an instrument of change, often used to steer or guide you and I toward a better life-altering path.

Real change often begins with looking back over real mistakes, misfortunes, missed opportunities, and missed destinations. Can you think of a time when an unwillingness to change was costly? I can. I remember dozens of times when my psychosclerosis, which is a big word for "hardening of the attitude" blocked my thinking from the right course of action. While we are revisiting memory lane, I can recall when my homeostasis, which is a big word for "doing things the way I have always done them" became very costly. How many more mistakes are you willing to risk at the cost of "hardening your attitude"? What is a logical reason for "doing things the way you have always done them when the outcome is failed results? Repeatedly! Come on, show me how intelligent you are. Show me how bright and intuitive you can be. You are not the person who wastes your most valuable asset—time repeating mistakes, refusing to grow, and quitting at the discomfort of change.

I am convinced that the process of change hurts less than the outcome of resistance to change. What prick have you avoided or continue to avoid? Physical pricks hurt. The pricks of change hurt as well, but avoidance is counterproductive. The prick of change is not physical hurt, most times, but instead is an invasion of our conscious, emotions, patterns, habits, etc. However, the sometimes-painful process of change is hardly ever greater than the painful regret of resisting change or staying the same too long. Would you agree? The more flexible you are with change, the less invasive and aggravating the process becomes. In light of the reality that you will experience change for the remainder of life, you must develop mastery in this area. Be like the butterfly and endure, persevere, and embrace what naturally occurs around and within you.

Pricks are often engineered to keep things moving. This is why the plowman would strike the ox with the prick. Animal lovers please don't get lost in the imagery of the statement. Stay with me here. I am providing context and emphasis. Pricks sting the oxen into action. See the bigger picture here. If the land is not plowed, no one eats. Everyone dies from starvation including the stubborn oxen that decided to quit. So, the one with the most wisdom decides to endure the emotion of pricking his favorite oxen to keep everyone alive. Pricks are invasive to our affairs until we answer their beckoning call. Think about it.

Have you ever had a nagging inner conviction about change, grew fearful of the process, and then finally addressed the prick and realized that the change was not so bad after all? I'm certain that you have. I have as well. This is how the process works. Fear is often the primary reason for a lack of change. Nevertheless, the remedy for fear is to move in the direction of that in which you fear. In short, act, and the fear goes away. The feeling of fear vanishes into thin air as if it never existed at all and leaves you standing courageously in the circle of change. J. Paul Getty, American Industrialist and oil billionaire said, *"The individual who wants to reach the top in business must appreciate the might and force of habit. He must be quick to break those habits that can break him – and hasten to adopt those practices that will become the habits that help him achieve the success he desires."*

Chapter Conclusions

1. The Prick Principle suggests that we are often aware of our need to change through what we continually sense within.
2. The word prick means to pierce with a sharp point, to pain, or to puncture. Change often begins with what theology refers to as a pricking process..
3. "Is there something eating away at you?" Is there something that is just nagging in the back of your mind? Is there something weighing so heavily on your heart that you lose focus when it is on your mind? Do you sort of begin to drift off into space when your awareness is aroused regarding a particular area of life, habit, or condition? If so, that feeling is the "prick" of change luring you into action.
4. From the words of Saul's very own testimony, we can see that while Saul was persecuting and destructively violating Christians, he was experiencing the power of the Lord's conviction inside. He soon was forced to acknowledge what he had always ignored.
5. I remember dozens of times when my psychosclerosis or "hardening of the attitude" and my homeostasis or "doing things the way I have always done them" became very costly. How many more mistakes are you willing to risk at the cost of "hardening your attitude"? What is a logical reason for "doing things the way you have always done them when the outcome is failed results? Repeatedly!
6. I am convinced that the process of change hurts less than the outcome of resistance to change. What prick have you avoided or continue to avoid?
7. Write down your strongest convictions or pricks. Meditate over them and resolve to address them immediately. Your destiny deserves the Prick Principle.

Courage is like love; it must have hope for nourishment.

-Napoleon Bonaparte

Dr. David McClelland of Hartford, an author of The Achieving Society concluded that your choice of a reference group can determine as much as 95% of your success and achievement in life.

-Brian Tracy, Author, and Success Mentor

Chapter 5

The Nourishment Principle

The Nourishment Principle suggests that it is necessary to be in a healthy environment that complements and feeds your change.

Just as courage needs hope for nourishment, your process for growth needs nourishment. Nourishing your heart, mind, soul, emotions, mind, dreams, goals, personality, etc. is a necessity for maintaining growth and the rhythm of change. After achieving a noticeable measure of change, it is easy to subconsciously disconnect from the source that creates rapid and stable rates of growth. The obvious soon becomes overlooked. Anytime someone is nourished there is a sense of fulfillment, relief, and even self-actualization. It is important not to misappropriate or assume that because we are mastering growth, we have fully matured. Greatness requires continual growth. The resolution or remedy is to commit. Commit to the environment that is producing the nourishment you need to fully change and transform into the greatness inside of you. Appeal to growth and not to a timeline.

Some of us relinquish what's nourishing us too soon. I am definitely guilty of this. We often become familiar with our support systems and assume that we have outgrown them. At other times, we become so comfortable that develop contempt where we should remain grateful. Out of impatience, ego, and arrogance, we focus on timelines instead of a thorough and honest examination of our motives. Therefore, we default to a timeline as the measuring rod for success. Timelines often function as projections and estimates based on intellectualism, assumptions, and pressure. Becoming one with the process will allow you to tap into the internal signals and changes that validate when we arrive at change. When I was growing up, I periodically heard the older generation say, "People don't have any sticking power anymore. You got to have sticking power to finish." Change requires sticking with the process and seeing things through to completion. Remember what I presented in the previous chapter about the 98% who fail at New Years resolutions? According to an article in Health US News, 80 percent of New Year's resolutions fail. Forbes reports that only 8 percent of people achieve their New Year's resolutions. What is the trend here? Little to no STICKING POWER. The issue here is sticking power. Even the butterfly changes successfully through sticking power. Can you stick and stay until you change? Allow me to explain.

The egg of the butterfly is placed on a leaf or root of the food plant. It forms a glue or sticky substance that ultimately changes the eggs' form in preparation for destiny and growth. So, the egg gets "glued" to what is nourishing and feeding its change. The egg has proper placement. There is an exact and proper placement for every season, stage, phase, transition, and change in your life. If not, you would not survive at all. There is a proper place for you to grow right now at this present stage, phase, change, or whatever in your life.

The place may be a company, a church, a friendship, a relationship, a geographical location, an association, and the like. The key is to learn to determine and differentiate a depleting place from a feeding place. Similar to blood suckers, ticks, and leaches, depleting places suck what little life force, energy, self-esteem, joy, peace, courage, dream, passion, and gifting out of you that you have as you fumble through the dimly lit seasons of growth. Ever experience any depleting places? Are you in one right now? Think about it. Take a moment to really be true to yourself. Are you going through a growth stage or change and one or more of your places is depleting you? You will not survive in depleting places. When I was growing up, the guys in the neighborhood had a saying that we used when we were about to exit a situation.

We would say, "Hey guys, I'm about to VAMP." If you are in a depleting place, I will tell you right now, develop a Vamp Strategy. In this case, A Vamp Strategy is a strategic, well-thought-out, prayer-based plan to exit the depleting place. Depleting places may not physically kill you, but they kill your energy, state of emotions, and your expectation. Do not just lie down like a rug and accept depleting places because you are afraid to take risks. You are already taking the scariest one-staying where you are! Please do not remain in bloodsucking, leaching, tick-filled places that rob you of your hope, dreams, and life force. People love comfort and therefore hate change because change disrupts comfort. However, discomfort is worth its weight in gold when your placement is attempting to kill you. Get to a feeding place regardless of how uncomfortable and scary the process is. You will feel so much better afterwards. Your hope will return. Your dreams will expand. Your joy will overflow. You will feel brand new. Feeding places are there to nurture the natural, raw, skills, gifts, talents, wisdom, goals, dreams, and purpose in you. Feeding places can be challenging because they often prune us but invaluable because they preserve us.

Feeding places promote joy. I have observed children at the infancy stage, and one thing that I have learned is that infants seem happiest when they are fed. The onset of new changes, phases, stages, transitions, etc. draws out our vulnerability. Vulnerability is good. It's a sign of humility. A friend of mine has a slogan that I find fitting for where we are in the journey. He would often say, "Humility is the wellspring of authority." Do you have any feeding places in your life that draw out your humility? Any places where you know a part of you is being preserved, cared for, and nurtured to the fullest? I do. My home is a feeding place. My church is a feeding place. My marriage is a feeding place. Identify your feeding places. Mark them. Cherish them. Seek them out. When you find them, hold on to them. Get all the nourishment from them that you can. Allow the feeding places to play a significant role in your growth to greatness. Placement is important. The question is, like the butterfly, what sticky substance can you or do you need to release to cling to your nourishing environment so that you can experience visible change?

Releasing the Negative

There are two categories in which we release or have need to release. We release both positive and negative thoughts, emotions, and actions each day whether we are in contemplation mode or not. Either release has the potential to work for our growth when carefully acted upon. When it comes to changing, we all have some items in our backpack of life that we are lugging around like nomads. We all have what I call "leftovers" from past experiences, both failure and success, which have the potential to cloud our perspective. First, seek to release the negatives. The negatives are obstacles, traditions, mindsets, and relationships that are often blocking our transition to becoming more. What are your negative narratives that you need to divorce?

You will know them by how much they distract you from goals, discipline, and being successful. As a metaphor to the butterfly egg, ask yourself the question, "What do I need to release?" Is it a failing relationship or maybe even a hopeless idea that has gone bankrupt? Is it a life-sucking habit that keeps draining your momentum, energy, or even positivity? Addressing this area can be tough to deal with. You may simply need to create accountability around you to identify what is blocking you from moving forward.

I really enjoyed learning what psychologists and therapists consider the four sources of negative emotion. The first is justifying. I found that justifying happens when we validate our reason for being angry, resentful, or whatever. This allows us to remain victims and hold on to our disposition or in this case our negative "sticky substance." The second is identification or attachment. Attachment happens when we take personal the actions of another as if they were intended or meant toward us in a harmful way. This often causes stereotyping, loss of friendships, missed networks, etc. The third is what is called "inward considering." Inward considering is overly exaggerating an incident in your mind in an offensive or negative way. It is telling yourself a story of injustice, rejection, abuse, etc. that does not really exist.

The last is blaming, which I understand is the most dangerous. Blaming is self-explanatory. If you have never blamed anyone for something that you should have taken responsibility for then you are an angel and should relocate from this depleting earth realm. Yet, we all have shifted blame at one point or another such as unjust blame on our children, spouses, friends, or employers. The truth is that we all have unjustly blamed someone for something that they did not deserve blame for. What is important at this point is answering my next question honestly. What are the negatives that you need to release so that you can remain in your nourishing environment? What is your "sticky substance"? Write them down and in a safe, controlled environment, burn them as a sign of getting rid of them. If burning doesn't work, throw them in the trash.

Go hard on yourself just for this exercise. You can burn the list later but for now write it all down. You know yourself best. Remove all shame and guilt. Meditate on it. Now, it is time to flip the coin. We have seen the negative stuff; yet there is so much positive in you that must be released.

Releasing the Positive

When I discuss release the positive, I am talking about allowing positivity to ooze out of you. I am talking about allowing it to gush out of your like a gushing fire hydrant. It is just as important to release positive stimuli – emotions, thoughts, and actions- in the process of change as it is negative. Releasing the negative cleanses out the feelings, thoughts, and emotions that block the positive from flowing forward. Once the negative is addressed and released, the positive is what we can use to "get glued" to the nourishing environment. If desired, you can be the most positive person that you know. If desired! Positiveness is not a secret trick or philosophical ideology. Positive is a choice. I am convinced that we are all genuinely good people. Broken at times, but genuinely good. Battered and sometimes confused but genuinely good. Underdeveloped, unloved, and even misguided but genuinely good. We were born genuinely good with plenty of positivity.

Smiling is positive. Laughing is positive. Loving is positive. We can easily practice being a positive person. Community is positive. Unity is positive. Good-will is positive. Productivity is positive. We may often hide behind fear, insecurity, stern looks, hurt, anxiety, shame, or whatever, but we are inherently positive. The challenge is learning the positive "sticky substance" to release into your environment in order to guarantee that you can nourish off of it until you are fully developed to move into the next stage. What can any of us release into our "feeding places"? I will pull my suggestion from the upcoming chapter. It goes without saying that we are all accountable for releasing love, joy, and peace. In addition to these three, I am also suggesting adaptability, flexibility, and predictability.

The objective in the feeding places is to *remain*. You will need to be adaptable to the sudden changes of temperament and personality of your feeding place. You will need to be flexible to manage the shattering ripples and quakes in the foundation of your feeding place. And you will need to be predictable, meaning consistent and committed, in your feeding place until you are fully fed for the next stage of life, purpose, and destiny. Release the positive "sticky substance" and get glued to the environment that is nourishing you into greatness. List all of the positives about yourself. Be extreme. Be over the top. Do not choose to be modest. Now, tell yourself that you have these qualities in abundance. You are a reservoir of positive characteristics. You will not allow the negativity of what's been to prevent you from what can be.

Chapter Conclusions

1. The Nourishment Principle suggests that it is necessary to be in a healthy environment or resource that compliments and feeds your change.

2. Appeal to growth and not to the timeline. Most people focus on timelines instead of becoming one with the process of change before them.

3. Even the butterfly changes successfully through its sticking power. Can you stick and stay until you change? Write out a one paragraph statement of how you plan to commit to growth in this season of your life. Post it where you can see it every day. Read and believe in it.

4. There is an exact and proper placement for every season, stage, phase, transition, and change in your life. If not, you would not survive at all.

5. Similar to blood suckers, ticks, and leaches, depleting places suck what little life force, energy, self-esteem, joy, peace, courage, dream, passion, and gifting out of you that you have as you fumble through the dimly lit seasons of growth.

6. List all of the negatives about yourself right now. Go hard on yourself just for this exercise. You can burn the list later but for now write it all down.

7. Release the positive "sticky substance" and get glued to the environment that is nourishing you through change. List all of the positives about yourself. Be extreme. Be over the top. Do not choose to be modest. You have a reservoir of positivity to invest in your nourishing environment.

We all experience moments when everything is perfectly ordered, but life is just not like that all the time. Things change. Life changes. You change.

-Bishop T. D Jakes, Author, and Movie Producer

To be flexible is to be able to respond to change without inappropriate attachments binding one to the past.

-Nathaniel Branden, Author, and Psychologist

Chapter 6

The Response Principle

The Response Principle suggests that it is necessary to develop the proper response for achieving a favorable outcome.

We often experience more small opportunities that lead to big opportunities, then we do big opportunities that lead to bigger ones. A wise man once said that the next dimension is designed to keep you out. How we respond in life is paramount to who we have the opportunity to become. The Bible records a group of amazing people who had experienced extreme suffering for over 400 years. This massive group of mistreated and underserved people were given the opportunity to be released from their oppression and form a strong and prosperous nation. There was one big hurdle to overcome. They needed to travel a great distance in unusual and uncomfortable circumstances while facing the threat of extinction in order to obtain it. Subsequently, they had the advantage of God's divine plan for their lives. Therefore, He miraculously watched over them while leading them to a great country in order to start over. Although they were free to create their own culture, society, history, and wealth, it wasn't easy. While on their journey to greatness, they continually complained about the travel conditions of the journey and moaned to go back. In the end, many of them never made it into their destiny. They never grew into greatness. They couldn't pace with the rhythm of change. In the end, others inherited their destiny instead. By now, you probably know that I am speaking of who the Bible calls The Children of Isael. Maybe there is some truth to the Response Principle. It is necessary to develop the proper response for achieving a favorable outcome or forfeit greatness.

In his book Six Pillars of Self-Esteem, Nathaniel Branden wrote, *"A clinging to the past in the face of new and changing circumstances is itself a product of insecurity, a lack of self-trust."* Change is the litmus test to determine insecurity as well as a lack of self-trust. How would you rate your level of confidence and security towards change? The answer is in your response or reaction. There is a right response and an utterly wrong reaction to every change experience. There is a saying that goes with writing books. The saying is that "content is king." If content is king with the finished production of an informative, inspiring, or entertaining book then "response is king" when it comes to achieving favorable outcomes. One false move in the wrong direction by hardening your attitude and the entire process to greatness can dissolve. When we are facing a career transition, one false move in the direction of stubbornness could cost a promotion. If starting a new business, one false move in the direction of "doing things the way you always have" can create a failed business. Believe me. I know from experience. If attempting to reconcile or even blossom your marriage, one false move in the direction of doing things the way you always have can lead to divorce. I am sure that you are getting my point here. Response is king!

Commit to the Process

At some point, in order to change we have to acknowledge what we have been ignoring. Ignoring creates a deeper well of ignorance. There has to be a step of courage that draws us out of pre-contemplation into the awareness of our need to change. This pathway can be the passage to a greater life, more consistent success, even healing and breakthrough. *It starts once we acknowledge what we have ignored.* For many people commitment is a curse word. We can say it. We can articulate its meaning, but we also despise it. We often look at commitment as if it is a ball and chain. Especially in relationships. You have heard it once and you will hear it again, "change is not easy." As a matter of fact, change is often difficult because change challenges behavior, habits, systems, cultures, and ways in which we have adapted. It comes against our fabric of comfort, ease, and convenience.

How would you gauge your level of comfort with commitment? How can you become more disciplined or become better at commitment? Our change pattern systemically goes from pre-contemplation to contemplation. Meaning that we have now become aware of the need to change but have deficient commitment. What you commit to can benefit you. I have seen some of the most talented people become bruised by circumstances, trauma, tragedy, and relationships. They walk away so emotionally battered, tattered, and torn that they despise future commitment. Commitment often comes without the comfort or convenience of controlling every narrative. It means that sometimes, its' not about us. We often have to be submissive and play supporting actor rather than the star of the show. Few of us like supporting roles, it is simply better to be the star of the show. The star controls the success and outcome.

Stars seldom get tattered, battered, and torn. Actually, the star can become more of an abuser than a leader and transformer. The star can become a deterrent to change rather than a motivator for change. A dictator rather than a developer. Stars often are failed servants and even greater failed leaders. It is only when stars add humility to stardom that they can transition into the roles of supporter or transformer. Rick Pitino, Famous College, and NBA Coach, once said of humility, "*Humility is the true key to success. Successful people lose their way at times. They often embrace and overindulge the fruits of success. Humility halts this arrogance and self-indulging trap. Humble people share the credit and wealth, remaining focused and hungry to continue the journey of success.*"

Committing to the change that you desperately need requires getting past hurtful experiences, hateful people, and hindering memories. This can only happen through growth. It requires change that comes from reconciliation, spiritual disciplines, unconditional forgiveness, mentoring and coaching, or personal and professional therapy. There are times when both are a necessity. Did I write that? Did I say therapy? Because the word therapy is another socially acceptable curse word in our society? The word therapy can kill a conversation, clean out a room, lock your conversation partner into a death trance, and even terminate a longtime friendship.

We need help regardless of how "alright" we have convinced ourselves that we are. Nevertheless, committing to change is the only way to experience favorable results. We can never complete where we do not first commit.

Rewrite Your Story

The topic of rewriting stories reminds me of Albert Bernhard Nobel. I am sure that you have heard of or read about Albert Bernhard Nobel. His commitment to changing the trajectory of his destiny is exceptional and quite divine. You may find that a little humorous once you read further. Albert Bernhard Nobel, born into a family of inventors and engineers, lived an impoverished childhood. Over the years, and due to his father's interests, the Nobel family began to experience wealth and prominence. Albert admired his father's interest in explosives and soon patterned his life's pursuit in the same way. Over time, Albert became very well-known around the world for his inventions of nitroglycerin and dynamite. Having achieved success along with a mountain of public criticism, Albert found himself in an awkward situation to say the least. From Albert's perspective the only resolution was…wait for it…you guessed it-change.

Ludvig Nobel, Albert's brother, died. The story chronicled that an obituary was released mistakenly naming Albert as the deceased instead of his brother, Ludvig. The obituary criticized Albert for his inventions and business affairs with explosives. It made him turn out to be a horrible person in Albert's eyes. After reading the premature obituary, Albert knew he had to rewrite his destiny. He didn't want to be seen as the minister of destruction. Albert soon donated his wealth to the recognition of noble deeds. Albert altered his destiny by changing his public image, personal pursuits, and practices. Today, the noble deeds of others are recognized around the world with the initial generous help of one man, Albert Bernhard Nobel. The Nobel Peace Prize was named after him. Albert Bernhard Nobel literally rewrote his obituary before he died. He made a commitment to change! We can rewrite the premature obituary that is being stated, projected, assumed, and even believed about us by honoring the Response Principle. Maybe the next big hairy audacious goal in your life will change the world-when you change. So, dig deep even if it means getting help for your emotions, thoughts, and behaviors.

Personal and Professional Therapy

You did not deserve to experience the pain, setbacks, rejection, abandonment and all the other dehumanizing experiences thrust upon you. You did not! You really did not! Woe to us who take ownership of the abuse and neglect of others. The worst mistake that you can make is to say, "Maybe I deserved it." Better yet, it is a travesty to see individuals living with the guilt, shame, and condemnation of hurtful and unpleasant experiences. This is not so much a strange or unrealistic occurrence. People do it all the time. Actually, maybe you have done this! Maybe you are doing it now! So, let me ask the question, "Are you taking ownership of someone else's rejection, mistreatment, abandonment or abuse of you?" How would you know? Have you checked your internal system to identify where your condemnation is coming from, if you have any?

Where your low self-esteem is coming from, if you have any? Where your identity crisis is coming from, if you have one? I have, and I found out that I had them all. They were all bolted into my mind and soul because of my father's abandonment and physical abuse of my stepfather. My narrative was since every man given the responsibility to nurture me was destructive toward me, I must not be worth anything. The near decade of brutal beatings I took from my stepfather concreted fear into the depths of my soul. I had so much fear that at one point as an adult, I would get afraid when babies stared at me. I wrestled with deep rooted fear far into my forties.

This hidden and sometimes unrecognizable state of life is embarrassing, harassing, and manipulative. Living this way will cause you to believe a lie. It will cause you to believe that you are someone less than who you are. Ask me, I know! I have been there, I have done that, and I not only have the T-shirt, but I also have a warehouse full of them. I have lived under this type of self-insulting, fearful, self-limiting, and demonic assault for nearly years. It started when I was only eight years old by a man that I call "Dark Evil."

You will learn more about him and my story in the next book, Born to Overcome. It is a true story of father abandonment, sexual and physical abuse, murder, and attempted suicide. Thus, the reason that you must not live in the shadows as a victim but find help like I did. One day I received a message from the least likely source that turned me in the direction of change. The messenger at the time was my nineteen-year-old son, the youngest of four children in a blended family. His message, though curtailed by his loving face and gentle approach, was piercing, "God wants me to tell you, Dad, that if you want your destiny, you must change!"

Wow! This was a humbling experience for me as I sat behind the sound booth at my church, and he stood directly in front of me. He was locked in a trance when he said it. It was gentle yet direct and laden with wisdom beyond his years. He did not have an agenda at all. The courage God gave him to say that to his father was a demonstration of God's love for the both of us. This moment changed my life more than I expected. My response was professional therapy. There was no way that I was going to miss my destiny. See, I had spent years of self-talk, reading inspirational and empowerment books, praying, quoting scripture and more. Make no mistake about it, I collaborated with the Lord for my healing. This was my spiritual and personal therapy. However, it became evident that spiritual and personal therapy was not enough to get me to the healthiest mind and soul available to me. There was still a brokenness in me that I could not reach alone. And I must say, considering all the baggage that I was carrying, together the Lord, my therapist, and I did amazing healing work.

This was not my first contemplation of professional therapy. Neither was it the first time I had entertained acting in it. My wife and I suggested that maybe it would be beneficial in times past. The problem was that I had never shifted out of pre-contemplation mode. I had never acknowledged what I had been ignoring. Nevertheless, once I realized that the entire weight of my destiny was predicated upon a much-needed change, I had to make the shift into action.

The value of my destiny outweighed the value of my pride and the fear of moving forward. Here is what I have learned about taking big, life-changing steps like going to professional therapy. I know. You are probably thinking that I am about to talk about getting over the shame, etc. No, that is not my point here although it is a significant one. My point is that you must first add value to change before you can possess the vision to change! Allow me to say it another way. You must see the value of change before seeing the change in you!

If you have been reading and following the discussion with my son and me, you would notice that my destiny was the added value that led to my change. Once I added value, which is worth and meaningful significance, to my reason for changing, I immediately stepped into action. Change requires the proper response and not just any comfortable appeasing one. What I did not tell you is that the following day I was on the phone speaking with a professional therapist. Now, my preference is Christian. I wanted the added comfort of understanding my core values as related to my therapist. Sure enough, I found a God-fearing, professional therapist with over twenty years of clinical, inpatient, outpatient, and ministerial experience. She was a perfect fit for my pain, personality type, and worldview.

Now, here is the deal. Both personal and professional therapy work. Try it. Success is in finding a perfect match for your personality type and worldview. Be optimistic especially if you believe in prayer and faith. I have learned that God hears and answers prayers. Want some good news? He will answer your prayers too. Maybe it is what you need to deal with those deeper core dysfunctions and issues that have the potential to keep you out of the next level, away from change, and only close enough to destiny to smell it without the ability to partake of it.

Nature is totally committed to change. Nature is obedient to shift at the appropriate seasons in order to show new sides and facets of her ability. What would happen if you made change natural the way nature does? How would your life's momentum change if you were committed to change? Nature changes exceptionally, continuously without failure because it possesses a few characteristics that we can adopt. Adaptability, flexibility, and predictability are three characteristics of nature. Try them. Practice adapting more than remaining the same. Practice more flexibility rather than stiffness or resistance. Over the course of my career, I worked for a global organization with a high sense of social responsibility, moral obligation, and Christian worldview, namely the Christian Broadcast Network. As a 700Club Prayer Center Supervisor, we had a saying around the Nashville site. The saying goes, "Blessed are the flexible."

Bishop T. D Jakes, Author, and Movie Producer, wrote in his book Destiny, *"When destiny looks damaging, be flexible enough to change so that at the right time, you will be positioned to get another step closer to where you need to be."* He wasn't wrong! Consider being more predictable. Practice consistency and commitment when it comes to seeing change through to completion. Maybe these newfound or polished characteristics will lead to your greatest act of change and your greatest success so far. Be relentless like the butterfly. The first evidence of real change is change that you can see. Visible change. The butterfly egg keeps feeding off of the food plant that it is glued to until its physical body changes. When it changes, it becomes a larva or caterpillar. Ready to crawl before you walk? In this scenario, it is crawl before you fly. For you will fly high if you choose to do so. Change sometimes happens that way. Especially, when we are attentive to the Response Principle.

Chapter Conclusions

1. The Response Principle suggests that it is necessary to develop the proper response to achieve favorable outcomes.
2. Change is the litmus test to determine insecurity as well as a lack of self-trust. How would you rate your level of confidence and security toward change? Rate it now on a scale of 1 to 10 with 1 being the lowest and 10 the highest.
3. Committing to the change that you desperately need requires getting past hurtful experiences, hateful people, and hindering memories.
4. You can rewrite the premature obituary that is being stated, projected, assumed, and even believed about you through one act of change.
5. You did not deserve to experience the pain, setbacks, rejection, abandonment and all the other dehumanizing experiences thrust upon you. You did not! You really did not! Woe to us who take ownership of the abuse and neglect of others.
6. You must see the value of change before seeing the change in you!
7. Bishop T. D Jakes, Author, and Movie Producer, wrote in his book Destiny, *"When destiny looks damaging, be flexible enough to change so that at the right time, you will be positioned to get another step closer to where you need to be."*

Vision is a clear mental picture of what could be, fueled by the conviction that it should be. -Andy Stanley, Author, and Senior Pastor

I think that the greatest gift God ever gave man is not the gift of sight but the gift of vision. Sight is a function of the eyes, but vision is a function of the heart.
-Dr. Myles Monroe, Author, and Senior Pastor

Chapter 7

The Vision Principle

The Vision Principle suggests that you must have a clear and concise picture of your ideal future.

Many confuse sight with vision. Sight is the ability to see what is before you. Vision is the ability to see what is within you. Sight can be lost when what you are reaching for is no longer within visibility. You lose sight of it. Vision is always within as long as you have the will and determination to access it. What is your vision? The better question may be, "Where is your vision?" Without vision, you have no idea of what to aim for or who you are aiming to become. The absence of vision is the presence of inner blindness. Inner blindness is a destiny debilitating, vision stealing darkness. Settling for inner darkness, whether spiritual or existential jams us into perpetual survival mode. Helen Keller, American Author, and Lecturer said, "The only thing worse than being blind is having sight but no vision." Helen Keller was the first deafblind person to earn a Bachelors' Degree.

Vision is also a matter of the heart and soul. It stems from that for which you passionately desire and long. All vision requires growth and development. This includes physical vision. When children are born, they do not have clear vision. Their vision is clouded. They only see shapes and forms. Over time and with some growth and development their vision becomes clearer and more definitive. As it goes for physical vision, it also goes for mental vision, business vision, life vision, prosperity vision, destiny vision, and all vision. Do not expect to have any form of vision without growth, maturity, development, and change. It is often change that paints a clear picture of vision. There must be change for vision to mature. Andy Stanley wrote, in his book Visioneering, *"For a vision to survive, it must be mature and healthy before being exposed to the cynical, critical, stubborn environment in which it is expected to survive. And maturity requires time."* His statement is inclusive of leadership vision, personal vision, and organizational vision. However, nurturing vision is a must for achieving greatness. One must grow into greatness through cultivating and appreciating vision.

What is vision? If you have lived for any real length of time, you have heard the word vision. Vision is a life, growth, change, business, success, and universal concept deeply rooted in secular, religious, and economical arenas. Everyone has talked, is talking, and will continue to talk vision because without vision you are going "nowhere fast"! *Vision is the ability to see a positive outcome or where you intend to be beyond your current circumstances or state of being.* Whether this is for self-growth, organizational stability, societal health, or community expansion, vision is necessary to achieve it. Possess a vision and possess an essential key to thriving, changing, and subduing in the seen and unseen of what lies ahead.

Vision is the ability to clearly see in your mind's eye where you want to be. It is the goal that then requires specific actions to get you there. Remember, it is your hunger to reach your destiny and purpose that gives nutrients to your actions to possess vision. How is vision connected to change and change connected to purpose? If vision is the transmission to the vehicle of purpose and destiny, then change is the gear shaft to get you there. In other words, vision and change must work hand-in-hand, naturally flowing together to achieve destiny and purpose like fish in the sea and birds in the air. Vision signals you when you are stuck at one level or gear. Therefore, indicating and screaming to you that it is time to change in order to get into the next momentum. Have you ever heard the sound of a transmission locked in one gear without the ability to shift? The sound is clearly identifiable. The vehicle begins to stall at one speed, and it sounds like something is ripping the motor right out of the chaste.

Shift Gears

Vision challenges us to change or to shift gears for the next level of destiny or purpose. Changing is simply shifting the gear of destiny to the next level so that greatness will appear. Choose your speed and go! Your speed is how well you embrace changing and then how good you become at asserting yourself into the equation. Why is speed important? Speed is a reflection of response time. Time is too valuable a commodity to waste. The quicker you invest in what you know needs to change and act, the more time you preserve for more critical tasks. There is a very common passage of Scripture often referred to by authors from various industries. It is written in the wisdom literature of the book of Proverbs, and it says, "Where there is no vision people perish." Vision captures where you are headed. You need a healthy depiction of possibilities and opportunities that come become nourishment for your soul.

Vision is a survival tool. From an analysis in the animal kingdom, we find that vision plays a vital role in finding nourishment for survival. Vision is a major factor in the prevention of extinction. I am convinced that there are transferable principles from the animal kingdom in which we can glean. Without vision, the probability of failure is greater. Without it we are confronted with the real threat of falling short of renewal, restoration, and recompense. How can you regain that in which you never took ownership? Vision feeds our belief in what is able until the manifestation of what you believe arrives. It is like an insurance policy. With most insurance policies, your insurance is activated when you sign the documents and pay your first premium. However, in a time before advanced technology and AI, your policy did not arrive to you until later. Though you did not have the actual written policy in hand, you still had the benefits of the policy. It was yours! You owned it! You paid the price for it. You might say that vision is a type of currency. Vision pays the fee for what you imagine until the appropriate time for the manifestation.

Vision Variation

There are three specific wonders in the animal kingdom with exceptional vision that in my opinion define the essence of vision variation. You will need variations of vision to develop the clearest vision possible for your life or change process. Most often, people have one type of vision and that is vision in what is ahead. Vision of what is ahead nourishes your decision-making capacity. Yet, you can lack some important lessons and practical wisdom along the way. You need vision variation to be great. The first species that lends valuable insight to vision variation, which is right, you know where I am going-the Eagle. The Eagle is commonly referenced when examining keen vision. So, what do we learn from the Eagle that can be applied to vision? How can a lesson from the eagle shift our vision while transforming for greatness? First of all, the Eagle can see miles ahead of its present location. It is said that an eagle can see a rabbit from two miles away. It has an extreme vantage point of microscopically pinpointing its target without any threat of loss or being seen.

The Eagle can also clearly see under water from long distances. Therefore, the eagle can search out the fish's location regardless of the aquatic barrier. That's an extremely valuable survival tool! The Eagle can approach its prey at speeds of up to 200 mph. Because of how rapidly it can move, the eagle has an internal vision adjustment system (IVAS) that allows its vision to repeatedly reframe the object as it gets closer. It's like incrementally snapping new pictures of the prey based on proximity. Wow! Are you able to adjust your vision as you draw closer to the destination? Adjusting the vision helps with projecting cost, energy, and investment. It is an adaptation mechanism that helps us become who we need to be in the present moment, season, or task. As we get closer to the manifestation it may require a better version of self to attain it. Clear and concise vision is looking far ahead into the future and identifying the target with pinpoint accuracy. Clear vision can see beyond barriers, like the Eagle can when fish is the target and deep water is the barrier. We must adjust for destiny, dependent upon proximity, timeline, and speed of approach. What is just as amazing as the Eagle's vision is the Tarsier's vision.

The Tarsier is a small animal found in the rainforest of Southeast Asia. The vision of the Tarsier adds amazing insight into what it means to have 360-degree vision. The first significant aspect of the Tarsier's vision is that it has clear sight in the dark. The Tarsier has supreme night vision. In the darkest situations, the Tarsier still maintains excellent, accurate vision. It can clearly see its target in the dark. Here is a characteristic of vision from which we can glean. When change produces pain, doubt, and unbelief, which often feels like you are in the darkest moments of life, choose to activate your "night" vision.

Choose to continue to tap into the vision of a bright and clear future. Hold on to it in spite of how dark life or situations may seem. Night vision has to become a choice for greatness seekers. Sure, it's difficult. But what isn't? I'd rather prevail in difficulty than succumb to defeat. Another condition of the Tarsier's vision is that it can turn its head 180 degrees, completely behind itself, to identify both predator and prey. How do we capitalize on this remarkable feature? Here's the application. Your greatness process requires being able to keep the vision alive before you while simultaneously looking back and learning from past mistakes. Looking back over life and learning from past mistakes improves your transformation percentage. In leadership and organization, we call learning from mistakes "failing forward." Whenever you can learn from failures, mistakes, mishaps, setbacks, and blunders, you develop into a more mature person along the way.

Another variant of vision is Chameleon's vision. You will love the ability of the Chameleon. The Chameleon has independent vision in each eye. In other words, the right eye can move independently of the left. Therefore, the Chameleon can look in two opposing directions at the same time. If you are over thirty, you have heard the saying, "Look both ways before crossing the road." Just imagine being able to do it without turning your head either way. Imagine safely crossing the road in oncoming traffic on both sides but never looking from left to right. At the same time in which the Chameleon is looking for prey it is also looking for predators. Amazing! Can you possess the ability to seek the prey or nourishment that feeds your growth and change while at the same time watching for predators or danger, pitfalls, traps, and distractions? Wow! When we master this ability, we are practicing transformation and embracing the greatness process at the highest level.

Pitfalls, dangers, traps, and distractions often materialize as people with ill-motives, opportunities with unrealistic results, and blood-sucking entrapment that destroy our plans. The most amazing factor about the Chameleon's vision in my opinion is that it can cause an object to be magnified three-dimensionally. Yes, it has 3D vision. Isn't that amazing? When the object seems too small or too far in the distance or obstructed in some way, the Chameleon simply chooses to use its vision to magnify the prey or the predator. This is such good stuff for teaching about vision. This concept translates into how you and I can practice magnification. Meaning that when the goal for greatness, destiny, or change become blurred – magnify it. What does it mean to magnify it? Vision can often become clouded, obstructed, threatened, or far in the distant future. However, you can choose to spend quality time amplifying the vision. Get locked into it. Lean into it. Breathe it. Taste it. Smell it. Think it. Dream it. Talk about it. Write it. These practical steps are all acts of vision magnification. Be the Eagle. Be the Tarsier. Be the Chameleon. Be willing to do what it takes to transform into your greater self.

Chapter Conclusions

1. The Vision Principle suggests that you must have a clear and concise picture of your ideal future. Without it you will fail!
2. Vision is also a matter of the heart and soul. It stems from that for which you passionately desire and long. All vision requires growth and development. This includes using imagination.
3. Vision is the ability to see a positive outcome or where you intend to be beyond your current circumstances or state of being.
4. There is a very common passage of Scripture often referred to in the Bible by authors from various industries. It is written in the wisdom literature of the book of Proverbs, and it says, "Where there is no vision people perish."
5. Clear vision is vision that looks far ahead into the future and can identify the target with pinpoint accuracy. It is vision that can see beyond barriers, like the Eagle can when fish is the target. It is vision that adjusts dependent upon proximity, timelines, and speed of approach.
6. The Tarsier has supreme night vision. In the darkest situations, the Tarsier still maintains excellent, accurate vision. It can clearly see its target in the dark. When change brings pain, doubt, and unbelief, which often feels like you are in the darkest moments of life, choose to activate your night vision. Choose to continue to tap into the vision of a bright and clear future and hold on to it in spite of how dark life or situations may seem.
7. Now, it is time to practice vision. Take some time at the end of this chapter to address vision. If you already have a vision for every area of life, review it, modify it, expand it, and embrace it deeper. If you do not have a vision for every area of your life-get one! Remember, sight is from without, but vision is from within. Where do you see yourself physically, economically, socially, spiritually, psychologically, emotionally, and relationally? Consider every area of life and write an amazing plan based on your deepest passions and beliefs. Then, GO FOR IT!

So never lose an opportunity of urging a practical beginning, however small, for it is wonderful how often in such matters the mustard seed germinates and roots itself.

-Florence Nightingale, Author, Social Reformer, and Nursing Founder

Change your opinions, keep to your principles; change your leaves, keep intact your roots.

-Victor Hugo, Novelist, Poet, and Author

Chapter 8

The Rooting Principle

The Rooting Principle suggests that you will find long-term stability and fruitfulness in the proper environments when you root there long enough.

Environments are critical. But what constitutes environment? Really. I prefer Merriam Webster insightful conclusion that an environment is the circumstance, objects, or conditions by which one is surrounded. I prefer this definition because surroundings are critical to growth, development, or disaster. The word surround conveys the imagery of being walled in on every side. Just think about that for a moment. It's important to closely scrutinize how we are walled in on every side. Surrounding cause our dreams and hopes to either live or die. Surrounding oneself with positivity feeds optimism, perseverance, and hope. A negative environment does the complete opposite. We cannot afford to allow our surroundings to choke out our hope. Consider this passage of Scripture about the criticality of hope. *Proverbs 13:12(NIV) says, "Hope deferred makes the heart sick, but a dream fulfilled is a tree of life."* Have you ever experienced a "sickened heart"? It happens when something that you're expecting delays over and over again until you grow weary and depressed. I have. I know what it feels like. And I don't ever want to experience it again. However, deferred hope is often directly correlated to our environment. Not only is the environment important for hope but motive is as well.

What we care about and how much we care about it can be at the source of a deferred hope. Do you know what this suggests? It suggests that the heart can be an "environment" that has become toxic and unfruitful. Jesus' said it better than I ever can in the Parable of the Sower. Explaining His disciples about the thorny ground in which seeds fall and are choked,

Jesus said in *Matthew 13:22(NIV)*, *"The seed falling among the thorns refers to someone who hears the word, but the worries of this life and the deceitfulness of wealth choke the word, making it unfruitful."* In my developmental process, I have often cared about material things of the world, influence, power, and more. I am sure that I'm not alone. I've just decided to hang on the cross here and practice vulnerability for the sake of your growth. The heart can be unhealthy ground to root our dreams, goals, and greatness. We often have to undergo "heart surgery," an introspective examination of our intentions," before really knowing what our truest desires are. Here is how we get at motive. When greatness is steeped in ill motives, revenge, and retribution we fall short of greatness that moves the world forward.

Environments are often the key to life's lessons, achievements, or failures. Where you are planted is just as important as what is planted in you. Your environment has the assignment of germinating, which means growing and developing, the amazing seeds of greatness in you. The amazing seeds of greatness must grow or change. Environment makes the difference. Oftentimes people wither on the vine of life, success, destiny, career, and dreams because they are rooted in a toxic, unfruitful, or unproductive environment.

Environments are jobs, pursuits, relationships, religions, mindsets, companies, etc. You cannot risk extinction simply because you have grown accustomed to being in a state of homeostasis (doing what you have always done). Most people follow the homeostasis patterns of others that have gone before them and live an unfulfilled life. For example, you may become a miner because your father was a miner and your father's father were a miner. Being a miner may have been their story, but it does not mean that it is your story. We often see this with religion. The father is a preacher, so the son thinks that he is supposed to be a preacher. There are occasions when this type of mirroring is authentic. Yet there are occasions when it is not authentic. In the case when it is not, the son grows up in an unfruitful environment that does not facilitate room to change or evolve into a true identify. Thus, leaving the son in an identity crisis which often leads to a life that flees from having anything to do with the church, religion, God, or mining.

Consider the condition of your growth or paralyzing environment. Your environment is the soil for the seed of change. Harvest on your efforts is directly and organically contributed to the condition of your soil. Author and Evangelist Joyce Myers once said, *"Consider a tree for a moment. As beautiful as trees are to look at, we don't see what goes on underground - as they grow roots. Trees must develop deep roots in order to grow strong and produce their beauty. But we don't see the roots. We just see and enjoy the beauty. In much the same way, what goes on inside of us is like the roots of a tree.* Change occurs in a habitat that allows it to breathe and create new life. Your environment is your soil! How do you assess soil to identify how healthy it is for you?

Assess the Soil

In order to understand rooting, you must first understand the nature of planting. Why do we plant? Planting gives life to the environment. The idea is for you to plant and take root in environments that create new and renewed life. This is the only way to master growth. They provide energy for the ecosystem because they can get energy directly from sunlight. Just as plants provide energy for the ecosystem, rooting in the proper environments provides nutrients and security to your transformation.

Planting is also an agricultural method of creating goods, economic growth, social stability, community development, etc. Planting takes on various shapes and forms depending upon industry, geographical location, or horticulturist approach. Nevertheless, all plants engage in the process of change. For whatever grows cannot do so without a change in structure, appearance, weight, etc. Planting is a means of preserving life. Throughout history every civilization, tribe, people, and nation survived through the agricultural phenomenon of planting.

It is amazing how you can plant a seed, of any kind, and if planted in nutrient-providing soil, it will bring back a harvest greater than the seed. Why? What is inside is always greater and adds more value than what is on the outside. You and I are the same. There is greatness in us. There is a butterfly in us that is greater than the caterpillar that is visible right now. And if you are already a butterfly, then dazzle the world with your extensive beauty, ability, and value.

When we plant in the right soil, we never get back the measure we planted. We will always reap more. Every plant, in order for it to thrive, grow, or change, must undergo a "rooting" process.

The type of soil in which you root becomes the environment responsible for producing fruit. Have you been in an environment that lacks the ability to advance your goals and dreams, nurture your gifts and talents, or even train you for the next stage of your transformation? I have. It feels miserable. If you have not, that is great. However, if you are rooted in an environment like that in which I have described, consider how you can impact the soil for growth or find new soil altogether. How does your environment complement or complicate your change and destiny? Meditate over this question. Write a list of pros and cons about the environment in which you have rooted. Remember, environments are places, relationships, mindsets, etc. Wherever a root can take place, consider it an environment worthy of assessing. The idea is to get rid of any unhealthy rooting so that you can move forward toward your awesome destiny and change. The change factor is life-changing for you. Give in to it and watch the manifestation of a harvest worth celebrating. Once you identify your soils then classify what type they are.

The Bible, one of the most revered and oldest historically written documents of all times, gives an analysis of the different types of soils in Jesus' Parable of the Sower. The Parable of the Sower, located in the New Testament of the Bible, is a story relating the four conditions of man's heart to receiving Jesus' words. The heart is considered the ground, and the words of Jesus are the seeds. These four types of soils in which the words of Jesus seek to take root and grow are wayside (beside the road), stony, thorny, and good. Each soil has significant meaning, yet the common denominator is that there is an attempt to engage the rooting process in all four. However, only one soil is compatible with the seed. Only one soil is nourishing to produce change and growth. I am sure that you know which one, but do you know how does it relates to your soil?

Life Soils

In the Parable of the Sower, Jesus speaks of the types of heart soil in which the seed of God's Word is plant. I would add to this truth that life also has soils in which we are planted as seeds. They are life soils. Life soils are environments in which we attempt to plant gifts, talents, plans, goals, dreams, time, and more. There are practically four types of life soils in which you can plant. The four types of soils are beside the road, stony, thorny, and good. One Bible translation of this parable says "beside the road soil" is between two fields. Well, that is not a ground that is plowed, watered, and nurtured. It is left desolate. It is literally useless for seeding. For example, beside the road ground can be a pond, railroad tracks, sidewalk, street, or whatever. In biblical days it was possibly an area used for commuting. It is not capable of receiving at all. As a life soil, beside the road ground can be translated as malnourishing people, jobs, relationships, associations, etc. They are unable to receive anything you attempt to invest in them at all. Surely, you have experienced environments like this. Environments where you cannot get anything done? Environments where you cannot progress forward regardless of how hard you try? If so, you have attempted to root beside the road. Refuse to seed into "beside the road soil." If it cannot receive you, relieve yourself of it. It is a wasted investment. The next soil type is stony. Stony soil are those in which you plant seed with an attempt to root but get nothing out because you cannot root. It is soil that lacks depth because underneath what is visible is layers of hard rock. This ground can fool you. One may consider it deceiving to the naked eye. Ever tried to grow or prosper in an environment that deceived you? If so, you were in stony ground. Nonetheless, what often happens is once you seed into these types of soils you see rapid or immediate growth. The problem with this is that it withers just as fast as it grows. Why? There is no ability to root. Therefore, if the seed cannot root properly, it cannot withstand the contrary elements around it.

I am sure that you have had an investment or two, maybe a relationship, in which you poured the seeds of time, treasure, or talent only to get a positive response that soon faded away. I know that I have far too many times. However, each occasion has been a learning process. Hopefully, I will not be a repeat offender. It is the most annoying thing, but that is the nature of rocky ground. It annoys because although it has potential, it lacks profit. You see the potential and you become convinced that you're in a nourishing environment for rooting. The problem is that underneath what is visible is a system, people group, culture, etc. designed to alienate growth for certain people. Do not waste time on potential without profit. Learn to evaluate environments for potential and profit rather than celebrate potential too soon. Celebrating potential too soon is an act of a novice who has little experience with life's soils. I've been that novice. Aside from overcoming rocky soils, you must overcome thorny soils as well. When you think about thorns, it sounds painful. Would you agree? In most cases, thorny life soils leave us wounded, broken, or bleeding out.

According to the Parable of the Sower, thorny soil are those that choke out your growth. Thorns are painful when, not if, you get pricked by one. I remember the first time that I bought my fiancé, who is now my wife, a rose. It was a single red rose. I thought that the rose was quite beautiful. I remembers saying to myself, "That's just the right color and size to make her smile." As I reached to pluck the rose out of the bunch of what looked like ten or twelve roses, I suddenly experienced a painful prick in my finger. Because I was in a hurry to finish grocery shopping, I gripped the rose with force and attempted to quickly remove it.

The pain was shocking. It caught me off guard. I did not understand. My mind could not compute how something so beautiful and majestic could cause such pain. I drew closer to the head of the rose to get a closer view. I saw the rose pedals clearly. I saw what I now understand to be baby's breath surrounding the ten or twelve roses. I even saw the green leaves attached to the rose. I could not figure out what caused the pain because nothing looked harmful until I gently moved the greenery around. There they were looking mean, ferocious, threatening, daring, and bold. They were thorns. They almost looked as if they were protecting the rose from intruders. I could not figure it out. How was the rose created to give birth to both the beautiful petals and the painful thorns at the same time? From this experience, I learned that life soils can be like roses. They can produce both beauty and thorns at the same time.

You are probably like me. You have invested or seeded your time, talents, and treasure into life soils. The life soil probably was a person, place, or thing that in one aspect was beautiful yet in other aspects, painful. Decisions, pursuits, and ambition have a way of bringing you into some painful, yet beautiful situations. Thorny ground also lacks sufficient nourishment for you to survive and grow. Although it has potential, it does not profit. Potentially, you can survive, maybe even thrive, for a limited time. Soon afterwards, the choking begins. This means that you can seed there, you can maybe even root there, but what you cannot do is harvest much there. Ever had this happen in your life? This is the most common type of ground in which we might find ourselves. Who can deny beauty when they see it? Although I learned the lesson about roses, that they have thorns, I went on to continue to buy roses. This is what we generally do. We endure painful situations and environments because of the benefit we are receiving yet knowing that they are still threatening, abusive, or dangerous. We seek immediate profit over long-term preservation. It is normal, so do not sweat it. The key is approaching thorny life soils with wisdom and caution just like picking roses.

The challenge is to recognize that your return on investment is at risk each time you revisit thorny soil situations. Your return on rooting or ROR is at risk as long as you seed in thorny ground. Maybe we continue in them without changing the situation because it is only a prick and does not hurt so badly. It is not all *that* bad. It is endurable. However, when you compare it to what you can have, which is amazing, awesome, life-changing, inspiring, revolutionary, etc., you are giving up quite a bit. Would you say that amazing is greater than not so bad? I would. If you have not noticed, choking is a tiresome process. When you choke, the life force is slowly sucked from your body. The oxygen and fresh air that you once took for granted now slowly eludes you. It is a horrible process to endure. The initial act is sudden, but the process is tiresome. Thus, the way it goes for thorny situations and soils. You can root there briefly. You can get just enough for a season, and it will not hurt that bad at first. Eventually, it will slowly kill your growth. So, assess your soil today before you suddenly choke, and your growth is stunted. Quickly get to good ground, which is our last ground to cover.

Good Soil

So, what are good grounds? Is it not obvious? Sure. Yet, it is obvious that we often overlook them because the obvious often looks boring, uneventful, normal, and dutiful. However, it is in the boring, uneventful, normal, and dutiful environments that we often procure the greatest harvest on our seeds. We reap the greatest rate of change and the deepest act of rooting in the consistent, hard, dutiful, uncomfortable places that lead us to destiny, purpose, dreams, and goals. Ease should never be a qualifier for success and growth. Good life soils are those that nourish our change and growth and lead us to harvest over time. They are often recognizable through the success of those who have gone before us. Winning big at change, success, goals, and dreams requires gleaning from other success stories. Most successful people will tell you that success is not easy but requires hard work, risk, failures, and determination.

Good life soils are those that have been nurtured by people with experience, knowledge, and patience. It is soil that affords you the opportunity to grow in the wisdom, knowledge, and skills necessary to groom you for greater success. The challenge with growth is that you may find it uncomfortable. If you can manage being uncomfortable most of the time, you will root in good life soils and multiply in key areas specific to your growth and change. You will always find fertilizer; some might say manure in good soil.

Dependent upon whether organic or inorganic, fertilizer or manure has an awful smell. However, it is a powerful agent for growth. The natural and artificial elements improve the growth process. With organic fertilizer, specially made up of animal sources, it is the one element of the planting process that presents a challenge even in good life soils. Yet by adding the growth agent to the soil, the process of change enhances, and the growth rate multiplies. Such are the conditions of good life soil environments. The change and growth process do not come without challenges, good challenges. Good challenges are those that help you and not harm you. They may be uncomfortable to address like manure yet if you can stomach the process, you can have the reward. Now, go put your hands in some good soil with fertilizer in it and grow! Fully participate in your transformation. You have to participate in order to evolve. Remember that the butterfly is inside the caterpillar. In the same way, the genius, marketer, techno-wizard, politician, mom, florist, doctor, and dreamer is inside of you!

Chapter Conclusions

1. The Rooting Principle suggests that you will find long-term stability and fruitfulness in the proper environments.

2. Where you are planted is just as important as what is planted in you. Your environment has the assignment of germinating, which means growing and developing, the amazing seeds of greatness in you.

3. Planting gives life to the environment. The idea is for you to plant and take root in environments that create new and renewed life. This is the only way to master change. Plants provide energy for the ecosystem because they can get energy directly from sunlight. Just as plants provide energy for the ecosystem, rooting in the proper life soil provides nutrients and security to your healthy rate of growth and change.

4. Have you been in an environment that lacks the ability to advance your goals and dreams, nurture your gifts and talents, or even train you for the next stage of success? I have. It feels miserable.

5. What is inside is always greater and adds more value than what is on the outside. There is greatness in you. There is a butterfly in you that is greater than the caterpillar that is visible right now. If you are already a butterfly, then dazzle the world with your extraordinary beauty, ability, and value.

6. Refuse to seed into "beside the road life soil." If it cannot receive you, relieve yourself of it. It is a wasted investment.

7. The challenge with growth is that you may find it uncomfortable. If you can manage being uncomfortable most of the time, you will root in good soil and multiply in key areas specific to your growth and change.

Times of transition are strenuous, but I love them. They are an opportunity to purge, rethink priorities, and be intentional about new habits. We can make our new normal any way we want.

- Kristin Armstrong, Olympic Gold Medalist and Author

Chapter 9

The Participation Principle

The Participation Principle suggests that you must take intentional and willful acts in the direction of your change.

The Participation Principle raises awareness toward the action stage. Action must be consistent in the long run to produce life-lasting change. Psychologists call this the stage of willpower. This is where people finally believe that they can exponentially advance, change bad behavior, effectively manage unwanted change, and conquer great feats. This is the stage when historically proven and unique techniques are applied to gain momentum. It is argued that at this stage, depending upon the technique, change can take place as quick as an hour or as long as months. However, when we are considering evolution into greatness, growth happens in season, stages, and ages throughout a lifetime.

Can you recall ever watching a caterpillar walk along the sidewalk on a hot sunny day? It moves so slow that we call it crawling. It's really walking. The caterpillar actually has six tiny true legs in which it moves about. It takes many teeny, tiny, little bitty steps or at a time. In reality small measures of change is the most successful approach. It is important not to bite off more than you can chew. As a matter of fact, when you are dealing with change, a little bit at a time is all you can sanely manage. Do not sit idly waiting on the fairy of change to do something out of nothing. Do not wait for someone else to blame for the failures and lack of change, growth, and success in your own life. Do something. Even if what you do is a teeny, tiny, little bitty step in the direction of change.

Change must be addressed in significantly small pieces each day in order to manage the new life, patterns, and energy being created. Jim Rohn, Success Mentor, and Author once said, "*Success is nothing more than a few simple disciplines, practiced every day."* Jim has mentored millions of people around the world with his practical, proven approach to producing new habits, peak performance, and success. His clients rave about great ROR, which is return on rooting. Many claim that their new habits, performance, and success yield high returns. The idea is to shift those who are contemplators into participants. Thus, the need for the Principle of Participation. Contemplation is often the beginning, but without action nothing happens for a contemplator. Anything can happen to a doer. Here is the tip of the day. When you are struggling with change, a bad habit, or participation, it is necessary to practice a concept called "swapping out." I learned this concept from one of my mentors, Darren Hardy. Darren Hardy is a highly sought out success mentor.

His fans rave that if anyone can produce you into a "doer," it is Darren Hardy. Darren suggests resisting the temptation of "resisting." I am sure that this initially sounds like a contradiction. Darren argues that resisting the temptation of resisting is too hard. Darren suggests practicing "swapping" instead of resisting. What is swapping?

Swapping is the process of finding alternative ways to overcome bad habits by replacing or swapping them out with good habits. For example, if you are a sweets addict and it is causing you issues whereby you need to change, stop trying to resist sweets and simply swap out the amount or type of sweets that you eat. If it is a big bowl of banana split ice cream, simply swap it out for two small morsels of chocolate. His reasoning is that most people attempt to overcome bad habits or make change through simple willpower when recent studies have shown that like a cell phone battery, willpower runs out based on the number or extent of challenge, difficulty, responsibility, etc. in a given period. Thus, leaving you depleted when trying to face remaining issues that require that willpower that you so desperately depend on. Will- power works, just not quite enough to go at it alone. Add swapping to your arsenal of tools that give you victory over change, success, and growth. The swapping method adds greater value to your learning curve by equipping you with more effective tools that become core competencies.

Are You Ready, Yet?

Participation mode commences when we are ready to take action and are ready to seek support from immediate surroundings. Immediate surroundings may very well be the untapped networks and the good soil in which you are rooted. The butterfly egg is placed on a food plant, but it is up to the egg to eat. Are you ready to eat? Are you ready to dive into the practical steps of change like a hungry roaring lion? Are you ready like an ambitious little butterfly egg? Are you ready to change into that beautiful, fantastic, talented, stunning butterfly inside? The world wants to see how amazing you are. Are you willing to show us? Well, if so, it begins with small steps. The success most people desire does not come through large leaps and bounds but through deciding each day to do a little more of the same proven principles over and over again. What are some small steps that you can afford to take to move you closer to the direction of your growth, success, and change?

Nathaniel Branden, in his book Six Pillars of Self-Esteem wrote, *"We can have clearly defined purposes and a reasonable action plan but drift off course by distractions, the emergence of unanticipated problems, the pull of other values, and unconscious reordering of priorities, lack of adequate mental focus, or resistance to doing what one has committed to oneself to do."* The answer to staying on track is taking the right small steps. Small steps begin with establishing goals and objectives. Sure, you have heard this a million times. Do you know why? The approach works. Setting goals and objectives for yourself is part of the small-steps-process to achieving your amazing potential and accessing change. However, goals and objectives have to be informed goals and objectives. Herein is where you can make your most critical mistake. You can lay out goals and objectives that do not align with your abilities, path, or resources. In other words, you can have uninformed, unrealistic, unmatched goals and objectives.

This is how you put the infamous "cart before the horse." This approach is the guaranteed way to failure. Therefore, do not set goals and objectives without preparation. Here is how.

Research

Research is critical to gaining the knowledge that you need to make your process of growth and change remarkable and informed. Research is what I consider a small step. It does not cost you anything to research. There are numerous ways to research how to become who you are seeking to become, how you desire to do in life, how to balance change, develop new habits, start new ventures, etc. Once you Google or search for your topic, you will receive unlimited results. Advanced AI technology have leveled the playing field of success. Research is at the foundation of successful management, entrepreneurial ship, investing, etc. As a matter of fact, research is at the foundation of what is called evidence-based decisions. Evidence-based-decisions is an organizational term and process designed to afford leaders with the best outcomes based on the research and outcomes of experts in the field. You never want to approach an idea, life-change, business plan, relocation, career goal, etc. without research. Research will give you the evidence or information that you need to take powerful right action. This is the same for setting goals and objectives. It is important to research before setting your goals. We're all out of excuses. Today's technological advances has tip the scale of possibility in our direction. The pendulum of achievement is more favorable for us than failure. Surely, we will fail. However, failure is more a self-inflected occurrence than other inflected one. How will you know if the goals will be effective to your growth, industry, and success if there is no expert evidence that applies?

Open Dialogue

Have you ever heard the saying, "The squeaky wheel gets the oil?" How about this one, "A closed mouth will never get fed?" I have. I heard the last one all the time when I was growing up. Probably because there was always a food shortage in my house as well as in the house of people in my neighborhood. But that is a different book. It is necessary to come out of the closet of guilt, shame, insecurity, pride, arrogance, stubbornness, homeostasis (doing what you have always done), psychosclerosis (hardening of attitude), fear, laziness or whatever and talk with trusting people about you and what you are dealing with and where you are attempting to go.

Progress requires vulnerability. Open dialogue may be the biggest, small step but it is still a small one that is free and manageable. The key to fruitful open dialogue is as I stated earlier, to talk with trusting people or people that you trust. There is always a foundation for our trust. Maybe we trust because of influence, association, reputation, or relationship. Maybe it is because we like something about the one we trust. Maybe it is a character trait or level of success or just that warm, kind personality. Whatever the case, once you open up and begin to dialogue, you will find that other people share your same goals, dreams, pains, failures, pursuits, and more. They are willing to share resources and ideas on how to approach your success, growth, change or struggle.

I guarantee that once you begin to open up just a little, you will soon open more and more. The next step in this process is to apply a detailed vision.

Write the Vision

Dr. Myles Munroe, in his book The Principles and Power of Vision wrote, *"Sight is a function of the eyes; vision is a function of the heart. Eyes that look are common, but eyes that see are rare. Nothing noble or noteworthy on earth was ever done without vision."* Your participation in any area of change, success, or progress in your life will only be effective when you invest in a vision. You should have a vision for every area of your life. In the coaching practice, in which I significantly enjoy laboring, we teach clients to develop a whole life vision targeting strategical and critical areas. These areas include every area that has impact and influence on happiness, success, and change. The key areas where you will need a vision are career, spirituality, personal development, physical fitness, recreation, family, marriage, finances, peace of life, living environment, and social life.

These are all areas whereby vision will keep you focused and on track as change occurs. There are times you will need to change, grow, and improve in order to keep in alignment with your vision. Vision is comprised of goals and objectives. Goals and objectives keep you actively participating in the development of your vision. Without them all you have are dreams, hopes, and wishes. The book of Habakkuk, an Old Testament book of the Bible, gives insight into the power of vision. It says, *"Write the vision and engrave it plainly on (clay) tablets so that the one who reads it will run. For the vision is yet for the appointed (future) time. It hurries toward the goal (of fulfillment). It will not fail. Even though it delays, wait (patiently) for it, because it will certainly come; it will not delay."* (Habakkuk 2:23, Amplified Bible) You are the runner. You are the reader. You must be the writer of your own vision. How can you run when there is nothing to read? There is no surety of a future without security of a vision. If you have not already, it is time to write down your vision. They key to accomplish vision is practicing what success psychologist call S.M.A.R.T. goals.

S.M.A.R.T. Goals

-J.C. Penny, Businessman and Entrepreneur once said, *"Give me a stock clerk with a goal, and I will give you a man who will make history. Give me a man without a goal and I will give you a stock clerk."* Although general goal setting is better than none at all, generalized goals will not produce the success and growth that you need to become your greatest self. The key to goals is making them S.M.A.R.T. goals. The S.M.A.R.T. goal concept is also a universal practice founded in leadership, organization, and success management development. As a matter of fact, the process is employed in most types of coaching such as life, leadership, professional, small business, spiritual growth and more. Smart goals are goals that are developed out of the need to help individuals up the rate of success in goal achievement. Here is how it works.

S.M.A.R.T. goals are crafted from an acronym. The S stands for specific. The M stands for measurable. The A stands for attainable. The R stands for realistic. The T stands for time sensitive. Thus, we get the acronym S.M.A.R.T. Make sense? Maybe not yet, but it will. A wise person, meaning one who carefully crafts goals based on expert information and sincere thoughtfulness, creates S.M.A.R.T. goals.

Setting smart goals is a small step in the process of growth, success, and definitely the change you need to progress forward. Dave Ramsey, Financial Advisor and Bestselling Author, wrote in his book The EntreLeader, *"Goals are the heavy lifting and cause the heavy lifting to occur."* Set goals that are specific. Generalized goals are too large. They are illusive. They are not thought through carefully. For example, if you say, "My goal is to lose weight," you are not setting a S.M.A.R.T. goal. However, if you were to say, "My goal is to lose 30 pounds in 90 days through working out 3-5 days a week for 60 minutes", now you have a S.M.A.R.T. goal. Smart goal setters get down to the tiny high value task that changes the landscape of their situations and create a high residual on effort. The key is to be as specific as possible. Don't worry about being too specific, you can't. Next, you want to set goals that are measurable.

Measurable goal setting helps us to gauge where we are in comparison to where we want to be. How would you know or determine that you have met the goal? What is the metric? What is the measuring rod of accountability toward goal achievement? For the example above, maybe it would be inches or pounds. Maybe it would be the results of a daily tracking sheet or weekly measuring session. Maybe it could be the ideal outfit or wedding dress that indicates that you have arrived. In other words, think like this, "When I get to blank I will know that I have achieved blank goal." Practice instituting measurable accountability into the goal setting process and it will transfer into advancement.

Set attainable goals. I like the Latin root of the word attain from the Online Etymology Dictionary because it has a wide variety of meanings. The Latin root word has a range of meanings including to attack, strike, or manage. It also can mean to touch. When setting goals, we have the privilege of setting goals that we can reach. We have to resist the temptation of attempting to possess others success, influence, wealth, and more. We have to focus on what we can manage. The goal should be to start with something within our own striking range and not the striking range of others. It is important to assess our own power and resources to assure that we are after something that we can attack. We become impotent when we seek to attack what we don't have power, wisdom, or resource to attack. This doesn't mean that we quiver at big goals and dreams. It simply means take one attainable step at a time.

Reassure that your goals are attainable to you. Base it on where you are in life right now. Do not go for the brass ring just yet. Brass ring attempts are for after you have achieved a significant measure of proven little successes. Goals need to be centered around what is within your reach until your reach expands. Then revisit your goals and write goals that are higher to attain. Set realistic goals. Do not say, "Tomorrow, I will be a millionaire," when today you are working for a clothing company making ten dollars an hour. Do not write this as a goal. Be more realistic with your goals. You will not miss anything. This will not reduce your faith or how you may feel God thinks of you. He loves you more than that anyway. Be realistic. The more realistic, the more you will achieve. The more you achieve, the more you will attempt. Now, let's discuss timing. Timing is everything.

A wise king named Solomon, who was considered the wisest man in history, wrote about the significance of timing in the book of Ecclesiastes. In Ecclesiastes 3:1 (AMP) the king wrote, *"There is a season (a time appointed) for everything and a time for every delight and event or purpose under heaven."* Our best plans of success, growth, and development will still only materialize at the set time. Therefore, we must practice setting time-specific or time-sensitive goals. Time waits for no one. Time adds healthy pressure and conflict to your attempts. Time is a motivator. Adding time to your efforts puts you in a higher percentile of people who achieve their goals. When you put time into your goals, you realize its' precious value. As a matter of fact, you can get back almost anything in the world except time. Once it is gone, it is gone. Become an expert at preserving time and what you do with it. This is a good place to add self-discipline. More people fail at their goals and dreams because of a lack of self-discipline.

Adding self-discipline to the idea of time-sensitive goals will keep you on track with doing what you need to do to change, succeed, and grow. Do not try to mark time. It keeps moving. Instead, mark action. Because it is action that often stops. Self-discipline keeps action in alignment with time's unyielding force of progression. Be sure to include in your growth plan other proven concepts. Some additional small steps for consideration are strategic planning, self-talk, mind-storming, prayer, listening to others, etc.

The Stigma of Hallways

The hallway between contemplation and participation is filled with great intentions but little action. Some people never make it out of contemplation stage and into participation stage. They get trapped in what I call The Hallway. The Hallway is the place between contemplation (thinking on what to do, having little to no intention of changing, weighing the pro's and con's) and participation (actually doing what you specifically need to do or acknowledging what you have been ignoring). If you are here, then my prayers are with you. Why? This is a dark, chilling, and scary place. There are some creepy, infamous personalities that hang out in The Hallway.

These infamous characters have been around for a long time. You have probably heard of a few. Let me remind you of them. First, we have Brother Should Have. He is in The Hallway. Second, we have Sister Could Have. She is in The Hallway. Aunt Would Have. She has been there forever. What are those other dreadful particulars laying around in the chilling, scary Hallway? Oh, silly me. How could I have forgotten?

Those are the boney remains of unfilled dreams. There is Mr. Untapped Potential. He sure looks like he suffered. There is a pile of failed faith. And do not forget along the walkway of the Hallway are the leftovers of broken self-promises and the sludge of I Will Try is plastered everywhere.

You are wiser than The Hallway People that I have mentioned. If you are in The Hallway, get out of that Hallway today! Commit to coming out. Here is how. By the end of this day, do one thing that you were supposed to do, said that you were going to do, or that you need to do that will catapult you onto the next stage of growth, change, and success. Remember that this act needs to be rooted in a S.M.A.R.T. goal construct. You may need to act immediately if you feel a sense of urgency at your core. So, you can come back to this reading later. Getting out of that Hallway is more critical than reading the rest of this book. If you are not in The Hallway but have cracked the door of contemplation and are looking down The Hallway at the door of participation-run! Run down that hallway and quickly get through the door of participation. This basically means taking massive action toward where you are seeking to go or grow. Change awaits you! However, feeding your faith and energy is critical.

Search. Eat. Grow.

Searching, eating, and growing is detrimental to the caterpillars' life. If it fails here, it dies. For our growth, the participation stage reflects the caterpillar stage for the butterfly. We both have the same three primary functions at our distinctive stages. At the caterpillar stage the future butterfly searches for food, eats food, and grows into a butterfly from that food. The soon to be butterfly starts out as a caterpillar on the hunt for its next meal repeatedly. It seeks to eat and grow over and over and over again. The caterpillar has intense focus on searching, eating, and growing.

In order to grow into its' greatness, it must live and breathe this process so that it can change successfully, achieve destiny, and sustain the environmental hazards. Following the caterpillars' pattern of change, we must consider mirroring its approach. We must search, eat, and grow. What does it mean to search? Search for the caterpillar means using whatever means available to find nourishment. Like the caterpillar, we must use whatever means available to get to good life soil or good environments that will nourish our growth.

Once the caterpillar finds good soil, it eats. It eats and eats like a growing teenager. I know what that is like. I had three teenagers in the house at the same time. What a grocery bill! Once you find the places, environments, soils, people, relationships, or whatever is feeding your growth, eat until you are about to burst. Absorb all of the knowledge, skills, insight, understanding, and more whenever possible. Be that person who is so focused on getting better that you lead the pack, set the standard, or achieve the award. Be the game-changer. Be relentless! However, beware. It will not be easy. Wherever good is breeding, danger lurks ahead.

Hallway Enemies

As a part of the script to the movie, The Wizard of Oz, Dorothy, one of the main characters, sang a song that captures the essence of the three enemies Hallways enemies. If you saw the movie, you will recall Dorothy singing this verse, "Lions, tigers, and bears, oh my. Lions, and tigers and bears, oh my." The reference to the three enemies indicated the real threat of getting to the destination. Such as it goes for getting to your destination of change, growth, and success. There are lions, tigers, and bears. Oh, my! However, they go by different names. They serve the same purpose which is to devour your opportunity for change and detour you from the destination or purpose of your life. The three enemies are resistance, rebellion, and repeating. As the saying goes resistance, rebellion, and repeating will kill your effort to succeed "in the water." They are deadly. Remember, you already have some scary, creepy personalities in The Hallway. Now you have to deal with enemies. Do not be alarmed. It's nothing unusual. There is always a threat against transformation.

If you were to research the word resist, you will find that it means to withstand the action or effect of something or someone. A synonym for the word resist is combat. This is what makes resistance so dangerous. It is combative. When someone is combative, they will defend against bad behavior regardless of its' incapacitating power. A combative attitude and mindset are sometimes impossible to convince or convert. Resistance pulls against what is drawing you into change. It is like working out with a resistance band. With resistance bands there is always force in one direction pulling against force of the opposing direction to create tension. Resisting change is what creates tension and stress. The resistance band are experiencing stress. The stress of the band makes it hard to keep pulling on it. When we respond with resistance to change we make the process of growth extremely difficult to fulfill.

The primary reason for resistance is fear. People often carry an intense fear of failure. Therefore, they practice complacency and apathy which leads to incompetence. Over the years, The second enemy is rebellion. Rebellion is awful. It is an awful characteristic to possess. Rebellion or being rebellious is what the God of Scripture called the Children of Israel. If you are not aware, the Children of Israel was the group of people that He chose to dwell among and deliver out of all of their captivity and sin. Moses, God's chosen leader, was called and anointed by God for guiding them out of Egypt and through the Wilderness of Sinai. The Wilderness of Sinai was the Hallway from Egypt to Canaan. The Israelites rebelled against God and Moses repeatedly. Ultimately, the older generation missed their destiny. They rebelled against change and growth. Whatever you do, do not become a rebel. At least not for the wrong reasons. I am not knocking rebels because I have been one before. I was a rebel for the right reasons. Rebels have made our world a better place. For the sake of our discussion, the wrong reason to rebel is fighting against necessary, fruitful, personal, and professional change.

A rebel is understood to be a person who stands up for their own opinion despite what everyone else says. The key here is that they rise in opposition.

This is exactly what the Children of Israel did in the case of Moses' leadership and God's guidance. They stood in opposition for their own opinion despite what Moses or God said. Rebellion causes you to turn away from what is drawing you into change despite what experts, authorities, parents, friends, or anyone says. It is basically another word for stubbornness. This is why God called the Children of Israel a "stubborn and stiff-necked people" in Exodus 32:9 (KJV). Rebellion is a biproduct of psychosclerosis (a hardening of the attitude). The third enemy is repeating. We are creatures of habit. We often draw back to what we know. It is our brain protecting us. It happens when we are attempting to get back to what is most comfortable. If resistance pulls you away, then rebellion turns you away. Either hurts your chances of growing into your greatness.

Why do we repeatedly resist and rebel? We repeatedly resist and rebel because of the pain and discomfort of change. When your pain threshold is weaker than your gain threshold, you will always give in to the pain. Your pain-threshold identifies how much you are willing to pay. Your gain-threshold identifies how badly you want what is causing your pain. You have to want it more than it hurts to obtain it. Some changes require that a measure of your control be lost or forfeited for the greater good of your success, growth, and development. Sometimes the process has to take the wheel and make you a passenger. Whatever you do, do not fall back. Do not be a repeat offender. Choose to endure the pain of greatness. You got this. Why? Why do you have this? Because you understand that you must search, eat, and grow repeatedly. You have a vision and a strategy. Remember that the strategy insulate from the propensity of failure.

Chapter Conclusions

1. The Participation Principle suggests that you must take intentional and willful acts in the direction of your change.
2. Do not sit idly waiting on the fairy of change to do something out of nothing. Do not wait for someone else to blame for the failures and lack of change, growth, and success in your life. Do something even if it is a teeny, tiny, little bitty step in the direction of change.
3. Small steps begin with establishing goals and objectives. Setting goals and objectives for yourself is part of the small-steps-process to achieving your amazing potential and accessing change. However, goals and objectives have to be informed goals and objectives.
4. Generalized goals will not make the cut. The key to goals is making them S.M.A.R.T. goals.
5. Have you ever heard the saying, "The squeaky wheel gets the oil? "Come out of the closet of guilt, shame, insecurity, pride, arrogance, stubbornness, homeostasis (doing what you have always done), psychosclerosis (hardening of attitude), fear, laziness or whatever and talk with trusting people about you and what you are dealing with and where you are attempting to go.
6. The hallway between contemplation and participation is filled with great intentions but little action. Some people never make it out of contemplation into participation. They get trapped in what I call the Hallway.
7. Some change requires that a measure of your control be lost or forfeited for the greater good of your success, growth, and development. Sometimes the process has to take the wheel and make you a passenger. Do not fall back. Do not be a repeat offender. Choose to endure the pain of change. You've got this!

When destiny provides the opportunity for you to get unstuck, heed the signal to change and take action. Adopt new behavior to get out of your small life.
-Bishop T. D. Jakes, Author, and Movie Producer

What we need to do is always lean into the future; when the world changes around you and when it changes against you - what used to be a tail wind is now a head wind - you have to lean into that and figure out what to do because complaining isn't a strategy.

-Jeff Bezos, Founder of Amazon.com

Chapter 10

The Strategy Principle

The Strategy Principle suggests that there is no success without strategy. In order to succeed, one must think through and strategically implement a proven plan.

An in-depth discussion about change without a winning strategy for change is just that -a discussion. Real change happens by strategy. Even when the strategy is not yours. Have you ever been the victim or benefactor of someone else's strategy? I have been on both ends-the victim and the benefactor. They both present similar tones. They challenge, mold, and guide the affairs and outcome of your life or business. Strategy is the core of a strategic plan. Strategic planning is a process of charting a direction for your life or business, identifying how to achieve the desired outcome through asking questions and research, outlining goals based on discovery, and then implementing that strategy to completion.

Do you have a strategy for your life? Are you living with a well-thought-out plan to achieve your dreams? When you are thrust into change by external forces, do you take the time to strategize before you act? Do you know that a strategy will empower you to overcome any challenge- internal or external? By the time we reach action mode, we are typically creating a strategy in our minds. In other words, you usually think through how to manage the change in your life or the desired change for your life before acting upon it. However, one key to a successful strategy is writing it down. Writing a strategic plan is more significant than you may know.

In his book, No Excuses, Brian Tracy references a recent study on why people fail at achieving their goals. He wrote, *"In 2006, USA Today reported a study in which researchers selected a large number of people who set New Year's Resolutions. They created two separate groups. One group wrote down their goals and the second group did not write down their goals. At the end of twelve months, they followed up on the responses of both groups and what they found was astonishing. Only 4 percent of those who did not write down their goals had actually followed through on their goals."* However, 44 percent of those who did write down their goals followed through on their goals. Do you know why 44 percent succeeded? It is obvious but I will tell you. **They were successful because they wrote down their goals**. They created a personal strategic life plan, and so should you. A personal strategic life plan is simply your S.M.A.R.T. goals on paper accompanied by your understanding, mission, and vision of who you are.

WARRIORS vs. WEARY

Change can be a battle. I mean a real fight with rebellion, resistance, and repeating. Wherever there is the potential threat of a battle, there must be a strategy to win. Sun Tzu, known as the greatest military strategist of all time and the author of the Art of War said, *"All men can see these tactics whereby I conquer, but what none can see is the strategy out of which victory is evolved."* Behind his ability to win wars and battles was his well thought-out and written strategy that took place before setting foot on the battleground. Strategy must be built on goals (smart changes) supported by your objectives (small steps acted out each day). A winning strategy, one that creates victory, is one that studies the enemy well and communicates the willingness to do whatever it takes to conquer. The enemy in this case is not "out there." It is not them. It is "inside;" it is the enemy within you. It takes a warrior with a mindset to conquer and win in order to fight with self. Fighting against self is a tough task and often requires a lifetime of effort. Weary people, those who are tired of wrestling to get better, defeat bad habits, or engage in change, never last long enough. Thus, in order to win, you need a strategy.

A strategy for changing the inner self requires three acts of bravery. The three acts of bravery are analyzing, identifying, and evaluating. Here is a simple approach to analyzing, identifying, and evaluating. First, *live in your reality not your fantasy*. Many people often live a fantasy life and not one of reality. They say things like, "I'm okay." "I can manage it." "No big deal." Others pretend as if they have already arrived and do not need to improve skills, peak performance, steward resources, or learn new concepts. In reality that is their fantasy. Our real-life status and outcomes say everything about the areas that require change. On the flip side, our current life results also communicate how well or not so well we have managed change and growth in the past. Our fantasy (the idea life that we have created in our mind) will trick us out of growth, change, and success. The Law of Belief says, "Whatever you believe with conviction, you will become." When you believe a lie, you live one. When you believe in a fantasy, you live one. I have seen it time and time again. I have even lived in my fantasy and made-up life instead of my real, ugly, collapsing reality. Have you?

Examine Deeply

Conduct a deep examination of yourself rather than a shallow one of others. In life, we tend to circumvent our responsibility by pointing the finger at the other person-especially when it comes to changing poor habits, unhealthy emotions, and the state of our soul. It is important to take wisdom from Jesus. During His discourse with the Pharisees in Matthew 7:3-5 (NIV), Jesus said, *"Why do you look at the speck of sawdust in your brother's eye and pay no attention to the plank in your own eye? 4 How can you say to your brother, 'Let me take the speck out of your eye,' when all the time there is a plank in your own eye? 5 You hypocrite, first take the plank out of your own eye, and then you will see clearly to remove the speck from your brother's eye."* In organizations this is a harmful practice of "passing the buck."

You have heard of it before. As a matter of fact, you have likely been the victim or perpetrator of it at some point in your life. Hopefully, this is not your present story. Until I read Extreme Ownership by Jocko Willink and Leif Babin, I had pockets of passing the buck and blame shifting in my life and leadership. Now, I am intentional about taking extreme ownership of failures and the like within my sphere of life and leadership. Passing the buck happens in everyday life as well. It happens in marriages, boards, churches, everywhere. Before laying out a strategic plan, I always suggest deep examination. In order for life to get better we must first examine our motives. What are the reasons for our opinions, beliefs, and ideas? Discerning motive must be intentional.

When our actions are birthed out of unhealthy motives, our plans will ultimately fail. It may take a while but sooner or later, our castle will come falling down. Jim Rohn said, *"Life will only get better when you get better."* Furthermore, The Law of Attraction states that, "You invariably attract into your life the people, ideas, opportunities, and circumstances in harmony with your dominant thoughts". Isn't that a great nugget of wisdom? Develop a rubric for identifying healthy motives. You have to score them. Look at motives on a scale of 1 to 10. 1 being lowest and 10 being the highest moral motive. When your motives are below an 8, you are in trouble. Finally, compare your motives to see if they align with your core values.

Core Values

What are core values? Core values are the values of your core. Core values are your innermost beliefs that are at the center of who you are. They function as a navigational system for who you will become. They are the reasons we become who we become in life. They are also the reasons why we suffer or benefit from what we suffer or benefit from in life. This is not always the case but most certainly can be. There are a broad range of core values. A very short list includes family, success, service, spirituality, prosperity, health, gratitude, faith, love, courage, hospitality, transparency, honesty, integrity, significance, and so on. Again, this list can be exhaustive. I have merely scratched the surface. Do you have an idea of your core values? Remember, they are at the core of what you believe. Value means worth, worthiness, or meaning. Your core values are the concepts of life that are most meaningful or have the most worth to you. Knowing your core values is critical to following the right paths in life that lead to destiny, purpose, change, success, and growth. Take a moment to consider your core values. Over the next thirty minutes meditate on what beliefs are most valuable to you. Right down the top ten values that you believe are at the core of who you are. Once you have your list in hand, narrow it down to your top five. Your top five core values are always most significant and typically lead your decision-making process. There are cases where we realize that we value something at our core that needs removal.

Eliminate Waste

In the core value process remember to get to the core of any dysfunction. Doing this first requires unearthing the shame of addressing it. Forget shame. Remove it all. Shame can keep you locked inside an inner prison when the key to your release is right before you. Shame can keep you out of opportunities. Shame will keep you down when life, God, and everybody else is working to build you up. Bypass the shame and get to the core of any and all dysfunction in your life. Work on it now. Check for areas in your life where you are tolerating what needs eradicating. Are there areas of life where you can respond better? Think about your career, stewardship, relationships, knowledge, spirituality, etc.

Ask yourself where are you entertaining chaos? Are you failing financially because of poor spending habits? Are you stuck in the same job because you are unwilling to grow and change? Be sure to answer from your reality. Choose not to answer from your fantasy? If you choose to answer from reality, you may conclude that there is dysfunction that you need to address. Unless, of course, you have it all figured out. And if you do, show the rest of us how. Because I have not yet figured it out, but I am working on it. What about you? Are you willing to work on it? Are you willing to change?

Back to Strategy

I cannot stress the need for strategy enough. Maybe because this is an area of high failure rate. Write your strategy! Your strategy is a huge chunk of your life vision. People cannot help you achieve what you cannot articulate. Those assigned to help you must be aligned to help you. Strategy articulates that you at least have an idea of what want and believe. Many success experts today suggest planning your business or career around the life you want instead of planning your life around the career or business that you have. They argue that for so long Americans have had it backwards. We have placed careers and businesses over family, friends, love, and making the world a better place. Looking back, we now realize that the things that we sacrificed are most important. I remember reading a recent study of a large group of elderly people nearing the end of their lives, the question was asked about things they had done and that they regretted. To the surprise of the surveyors, the elderly group talked more about how they regretted what they did not do instead of what they did do.

I remember when I enrolled in an Insane Productivity seminar, hosted by Darren Hardy, Publisher of Success Magazine. During one of the modules, Darren talks about the concept of a whole life plan. According to Darren, who is an Entrepreneur and Success Mentor as well, your life plan should be detailed and specific. For example, decide what pay scale you want. List the type of home. Define what neighborhood. Talk about your vacations, where, and how many times a year. Discuss what type of company you would like to build a career with or what specific products and services you want to offer to clients. Discuss your family size. Identify how many children you want and whether you want boys, girls, or both. Are you getting the picture?

Aside from the above-mentioned ideas, your whole life plan will flourish if you add a few other elements. In your whole life plan or strategy, decide what your value or monetary worth is. Identify to what your hourly dollar value equates.

This will help you identify how to best allocate your time. If not, you will waste time on low value tasks that do not equate to your hourly value. Here a simple strategy. Take the annual salary that you would like to make and divide it by 2000 hours. Here is an old formula that I've learned over the years. I am not sure who authored it, but it has been in circulation for quite some time. There are 52 weeks in a year. On average you work 40 hours per week. When you multiply the two numbers you average about 2000 hours. Now take your annual salary and divide it by 2000. This will give you what you are worth per hour. For example, if you intend to make $100,000 per year you are worth $50 per hour.

Here are a few questions to consider. What are your top 3 skills that create success? What is the one thing that you do best? Where are you attempting to go in life? How far? Who are you aiming to become? Who are the key players around you to aid in achieving your goals? What skills do you offer your employer or clients? What skills do you need to gain?

What resources do you need to succeed? What key results are you seeking? By what rubric or metrics are you gauging success, change, and growth? How flexible are you willing to be with your strategy? How can you do fewer things, better, with less time? Be relentless with your strategy. Think it. Write it. Believe it. Work it. It will work for you.

Chapter Conclusions

1. The Strategy Principle suggests that there is no success without strategy..

2. Strategy is the core of a strategic plan. Strategic planning is a process of charting a direction for your life or business, identifying how to achieve the desired outcome through asking questions and research, outlining goals based on discovery, and then implementing that strategy to completion. Do you have a strategy for your life?

3. In his book, No Excuses, Brian Tracy references a recent study on why people fail at achieving their goals. He wrote, "In 2006, USA Today reported a study in which researchers selected a large number of people who set New Year's Resolutions. At the end of twelve months, they followed up on the responses and what they found was astonishing. Only 4 percent of those who did not write down their goals had actually followed through with their goals." (MJF Books, 2010)

4. A strategy for changing the inner me requires three acts of bravery. The three acts of bravery are analyzing, identifying, and evaluating self.

5. Take a moment to consider your core values. Over the next thirty minutes meditate on what beliefs are most valuable to you. Right down the top ten values that you believe are at the core of who you are. Once you have your list in hand, narrow it down to your top five.

6. Write your strategy! Your strategy is a huge chunk of your life vision. People cannot help you achieve what you cannot articulate.

7. Be relentless with your strategy. Think it. Write it. Believe it. Work it. It will work for you.

If you know the enemy and know yourself, you need not fear the results of a hundred battles.

-Sun Tzu, Author, and Military Strategist

The enemy is within the gates; it is with our own luxury, our own folly, our own criminality that we have to contend.

-Marcus Tullius Cicero, Roman Philosopher and Orator

Chapter 11

The Enemy Principle

The Enemy Principle suggests that wherever there is organic growth, enemies seek to destroy.

Anywhere there is organic growth, there is the threat of enemies. If a person, place, or thing is growing, there is also potential for poisons, weeds, and predators. Growth is organic. Anytime natural, raw, untainted growth is sprouting and blooming, pollutants tend to feed off of and attach to that growth. Growth is the process where good and bad compete because everything is fighting to live and no one or nothing seeks to die. All of life is self-preserving. So, if you do not plan and prepare for a way to deal with enemies like poisons, weeds, and predators, you may still fail regardless of how hard you work or how good of a job you have done at growing and changing. Let's compare the Enemy Principle to the concept of growing vegetation and the marketplace.

Consider the common use of pesticides. Certain pesticides or protectants are chemically and naturally designed to prevent weeds, pollutants, and other predators from destroying what is organically growing. Companies deploy strategic measures that are used to prevent contaminating ideas, inventions, etc. They are called securities, policies and procedures, firewalls, board or directors, compliance officers, EEOC, to name a few. These are common securities designed to proactively attack the production of toxic environments and predators in the marketplace from destroying healthy change and growth. If vegetation and the marketplace require a plan for enemies of change and growth such as predators, weeds, and poisons, so should your whole-life plan. It is the way to protect your dreams from collapse.

What is your toxicity avoidance strategy? What measures, systems, ideas, and accountability can you put in place to prevent toxic choke holds and invasive predatory attacks on your destiny, success, and journey into the next level or dimension of vision, change, and purpose? Who or what is guarding the gates of your great city in which you are trying to build? Identify what can be considered toxic, poisonous, or damaging to your growth, change, or success. What are the predators that have devoured your growth, plans, and dreams in the past? Maybe they exist now! Locate them mentally, literally, and figuratively. Now write them down. List them all-big and small. Every enemy of your change, growth, and success must be quarantined or destroyed. How can you avoid them? How did you avoid them before? Did your previous approach work? How and why? Answer the tough question and you will develop a winning plan to eradicate them today. Once you identify them, here is what is next. Avoidance. That is correct. I used the big "A" word that we often shame and tag as a no-no. Yet, in this case, avoidance is an excellent proactive plan to eliminate toxicity in your growth and change plan. What are the typical toxins and predators to your change and growth? I am basically emphasizing that you have a specific role to play in what you achieve, how you grow, and what changes you make in life. It's not going to happen by osmosis.

Avoid Self-Destructive Habits

We, as stated by Marcus Tullius Cicero, can often be our greatest enemy, our most pollutant toxin, and our life choking weed. We are our own greatest contaminant, toxin, poison, and predator of vision, dreams, passions, goals, etc. No one else but us! Here is a quote that I live by, *"In life it's not about what happens to you but how YOU respond to life"* (Author Unknown). We are responsible for our own responses regardless of what is thrust upon us. If not, we fall into the dangerous trap of blaming others. Blame has been identified by psychologists as the number one most dangerous negative emotion. The reason for this is because blaming is linked to violence, aggression, and apathy. When you blame someone else for your life situation, you tend to victimize yourself, paralyze your growth, and stabilize long-term anger in your life. Someone has hurt, misused, mistreated, disrespected, and overlooked you. Yes. I am sure. However, you are responsible for developing the capacity to respond in a healthy and productive manner. If not for any other reason, for your own sanity and peace.

Life is filled with precious and destructive moments. As a matter of fact, the destructive moments are more like horrifying nightmares set on "repeat"! Nevertheless, no matter how much you are plagued with circumstances that reflect other horrific moments or setbacks in your life, it is still up to you to determine what response produces the most delicious, sweet fruit. Not literal fruit, of course, but fruit of success, victory, and preservation. What type of toxins do we project? We produce toxins knowingly and unknowingly. Procrastination, meaning waiting around for things to just happen or to come to fruition out of osmosis, is a toxin that we often unknowingly produce. I will tell you now, osmosis is not a success concept for achieving destiny, purpose, or behavior change. According to Google Dictionary, osmosis is the process of gradual or unconscious assimilation of ideas, knowledge, etc. It has significance in biology and chemistry but not in the chemistry of creating lasting success and change. Second, we tend to talk our way out of change and success. The misuse or ill-use of words can lead to a toxic, poisonous, and violent assault on our success. Because what we say is powerful. How are your words lately?

Words Matter

I think the words of Yehuda Berg speak well on this subject. The Rabbi and Best-selling Author once said, *"Words are singularly the most powerful force available to humanity. We can choose to use this force constructively with words of encouragement, or destructively using words of despair. Words have energy and power with the ability to help, to heal, to hinder, to hurt, to harm, to humiliate and to humble."* Wow! What another nugget of wisdom to adopt. Berg is not the author of this wisdom. He simply knows that value of it. Words of destruction are not wording that appeal to the nature of your change or success. I often say, *"Words are your personal construction company. They are like hands released from your mouth with the license to either construct or deconstruct your destiny"!* If you love the Bible as I do, you will find life and transformation in this New Testament.

Matthew 15:11(NASB 1995) says, *"It is not what enters into the mouth that defiles the man, but what proceeds out of the mouth, this defiles the man."*

Words are so powerful. They create our internal story. One of my favorite teachings on speech is found in the book of Proverbs. Proverbs is known for its' many wise sayings. Proverbs 15:4 (MSG) says, "Kind words heal and help; cutting words wound and maim." What we say to ourselves make up our internal story. Your internal story is a composite of all the negative and positive circumstances that you have experienced through childhood and what you're saying inside about them. It makes up your self-concept which is comprised of your self-esteem, self-ideal, and self-image. Thus, the words that you say within yourself are just as destructive as the words that you speak aloud. The process works the same from a constructive perspective as well. The positive, life-transforming words that you speak aloud will draw an awesome and magnificent life for you both internally and externally. This is why you should develop a pattern or habit of what success mentors and achievers call positive "self-talk."

Self-talk is the simple concept of becoming your own cheerleader and motivator. Self-talk is a barrier to self-limiting beliefs. It is the concept of self-encouragement. There is nothing wrong or weird about talking to yourself at all. I do it all the time. Learn to do this as much as possible and you will be amazed at how good it makes you feel. Self-talk is a confidence booster. As we bridle our tongues to charter a course toward sailing into our greatness, we achieve success quicker. Benjamin Franklin said, *"Without continual growth and progress, such words as improvement, achievement, and success have no meaning."*

For every client that I mentor for success, I start with the internal story. Before I begin attempting to help them construct an ideal future, I must first identify what has been erected by their self-talk. Otherwise, I am attempting to help them build on top of what could be an unstable foundation. Regardless of who they are, how much power they have or think they have, or how much they think they know, I start everyone, and I mean everyone with their internal story. It is important for me to identify their understanding and state of self-esteem, self-ideal, and self-image. Then, together, we begin the rewiring process. You can always rewire your self-concept circuit board. You can always rewrite your internal story. Each client that submits to this process grows in life-changing ways.

You would be surprised how often we tell ourselves a negative internal story. One scene of your life's play that is written negatively through negative self-talk can set you at a disadvantage in your confidence, courage, and character. Think about it. Words are critical. Monitor them well. Proverbs 18:20-21(CSB) says, *"From the fruit of their mouth a person's stomach is filled; with the harvest of their lips, they are satisfied. The tongue has the power of life and death, and those who love it will eat its fruit."* In other words, you will become and or do what you are saying within yourself. In essence, your outer world is a reflection of your inner world. Again, this favors the Law of Attraction which says you will attract into your life that which is of your most dominant thoughts.

Purging the toxins in our speech provide us with reasonable insight into a healthier internal story.

Eliminating Toxins

There are a number of internal toxins that can prohibit organic growth, change, and success in your life. They can also keep you in a state of psychosclerosis (hardening of attitude) or homeostasis (repeating what you have always done). They can be a soft nudge or whispering voice. They can also materialize as a loud yell from a rooted issue. A lack of forgiveness is at the top of the list of negative internal toxins. I once read that to forgive others is the most selfish act on the planet because it is all about the person doing the forgiving. Of course, this statement is one that is intended to highlight the benefits of forgiveness. We all understand that forgiving others is far from selfish. People often conclude that if they do not forgive the person who hurt or offended them, then they are making them pay for what they have done. Wrong. This is so far from the truth. When you fail to forgive, you are actually holding yourself hostage to situations and acts that hurt you. The perpetrated has often moved on with life while the victim holds on to the residue of their hurt and trauma. If our perpetrators had any real sense of how precious we are to the world, they would never have harmed us.

As it goes for the caterpillar, so it goes for us. The caterpillar has to beware of toxins and predators. These are not enemies that lie within but enemies that lie without. What about external toxins and predators from without? Predators are more external. Pesticides are toxic to caterpillars, but birds and wasps are their predators. We have to know what our toxins and predators are. Toxins eat at you slowly. They kill you from the inside out while predators hunt you down and destroy you bite by bite and tear you limb from limb. Your toxins and your predators are in your nourishing environment; you just have to watch out that you do not get sprayed and watch out that you do not get eaten. Notice that the toxins are the substances that get you, but the predators are the living forces that get you. What substances exist such as smoking, overeating, drugs, overconsumption of alcohol, television, gossip, etc. that usually kill your growth and development from the inside out? Stop now and be honest with yourself. Make a list of every substance that is depleting you from growing. What are your enablers? What pesticide is out to destroy your growth? What are your toxins? We are all overcoming some. Now, make a commitment to do one thing. STOP, even if you need to get professional help. STOP. What living forces such as friends, associates, enemies, and people around you are ripping you limb from limb? Not literally, but rather taring out your heart with betrayal, drama, and confrontation.

I love listening to the teaching of great leaders especially those who have influence into the lives of millions. Due to experience and exposure some of their wisdom is layered and saturated with insight. One international leader, philanthropist, and entrepreneur whose teachings I enjoy is Bishop Thomas Dexter Jakes. I am quite sure you know him or have heard of him. If not, you have really been living under a rock and need to diversify your base of influencers. Nevertheless, while listening to one of his teachings on relationships, I gleaned a nugget of wisdom into how you can allow predators in the form of people with ill intent to destroy you.

Jakes taught that there are three types of people that we willingly allow into our circle of influence. He argues that the three types of people are confidants, constituents, and comrades. Confidants last over our entire lifetime. They are people who will "ride or die with us." They stick through the mountains and valleys of life. Keep these people near and dear to you. They will help you get through the roughest times in life and faithfully celebrate your accomplishments. Constituents are those people who are for the same things that you are. They are not lifelong friends. They are not "ride or die" people. They are only there for the common cause that you both share. The challenge here is to learn to differentiate a constituent from a comrade because they both respond and support you in very similar ways. They carry similar character traits. However, constituents laugh and smile with you as long as you are achieving the goal to their satisfaction.

The true test of loyalty occurs when a "quicker route to the goal" appears. Constituents will leave you or "bleed" (hurt emotionally) you when a better alternative to the common goals come along. I have made the mistake of embracing constituents as confidants a million times. Oh, and it hurts badly. It cuts very deep. I know that you have been there before. We all have. You just have to learn to care for your wounds, heal, and start from scratch. What about comrades? This one is the simplest. Comrades are people who fight for the same things for which you fight. They are not exactly for what you are for. However, they just fight what you fight. In other words, you share a common enemy. Thus, when the enemy is defeated, you both part ways. Now, make a list of people in your life and divide them into three categories. Who are your confidants? Who are your constituents? Who are your comrades? After completing this list, identify the predators and immediately begin to hide from predators if you want to avoid being eaten alive.

Chapter Conclusions

1. The Enemy Principle suggests that wherever there is organic growth, enemies seek to destroy. You must beware of toxins and predators to organic growth and change.

2. Anytime natural, raw, untainted growth is sprouting and blooming, pollutants tend to feed off of and attach to that growth. Growth is the process where good and bad compete because everything is fighting to live and no one or nothing seeks to die.

3. What is your toxicity removal strategy? What measures, systems, ideas, and accountability can you put in place to prevent toxic choke holds and invasive predatory attacks on your destiny, success, and journey?

4. As Marcus Tullius Cicero stated, we can often be our greatest enemy, our most pollutant toxin, and our most choke-natured weed. We are the greatest contaminant, toxin, poison, and predator of our vision, dreams, passions, goals, etc. No one else! Here is a quote for you, *"In life it's not about what happens to you but how YOU respond to life"* (Author Unknown).

5. The Rabbi and Best-selling Author Yehuda Berg once said, *"Words are singularly the most powerful force available to humanity. We can choose to use this force constructively with words of encouragement, or destructively using words of despair. Words have energy and power with the ability to help, to heal, to hinder, to hurt, to harm, to humiliate and to humble."*

6. What substances exist in your life such as smoking, overeating, drugs, overconsumption of alcohol, television, gossip, etc. Remember that they usually kill our growth and development from the inside-out? Stop now and be honest with yourself. Make a list of every substance that is depleting you from growing. What are your enablers? What pesticide is out to destroy your growth? What are your toxins? We are all overcoming some. Now, make a commitment to do one thing. STOP, even if you need to get professional help. STOP.

7. Make a list of people in your life and divide them into three categories. Who are your confidants? Who are your constituents? Who are your comrades? After completing this list, identify the predators and immediately begin to hide from predators if you want to avoid being eaten alive.

We must all suffer from one of two pains: the pain of discipline or the pain of regret. The difference is discipline weighs ounces while regret weighs tons.
-Jim Rohn, Success Mentor and Author

...Our need for immediate gratification can turn us into the most reactive, non-thinking animals around.
-Darren Hardy, Success Mentor and Author

Chapter 12

The Self-Discipline Principle

The Self-Discipline Principle suggests that mastering self-discipline in your life is necessary for fulfilling your goals and sustaining a focused path.

Considering his expansive background as a successful mentor and leader and the fact that he devoted an entire book to the mastery of self-discipline in every area of your life, I must refer to Brian Tracy's excellent and stimulating observations. In his book, No Excuses, Brian Tracy reveals an overabundance of benefits to learning and applying the skill of self-discipline. I must admit, I am like most people. The term self-discipline is kind of unsettling. It makes me think boring, laborious, tedious, strict, and the like. I am more of a free spirit type. You probably have similar thoughts as I do. However, I have learned, and so have you that self-discipline is a substantial ingredient to success, change, destiny, and growth. Tracy argues that *self-discipline is the ability to do what you should do, when you should do it, whether you feel like it or not.*

There is a chapter is his book titled, The Miracle Of Self-Discipline. In short, self-discipline requires the mastery of self-control, self-denial, and delayed gratification. Whew! I feel my temperature rising right now. These are all words that many do not want to hear on a regular basis. We live in a society and have for the last 50 years where most anything is accessible at the click of a button or a dial of a phone. We are a society of immediate gratification and not delayed gratification. Yet, to be great, the caterpillar must practice self-discipline. The process to change is slow, methodical, and structured.

Napoleon Hill, author of the book Think and Grow Rich, which has sold over 15 million copies said, *"Self-discipline is the master key to riches."*

Mastering your behavior is ultimately the key to successful change. When you can channel your energies down the canal of your destiny one stable, calm, focused stroke at a time, you will get there. Most things that we attempt in life require repetition. Psychologists believe that this creates groves in our neural pathways that help the brain recognize what we are exercising as a habit. If repeated 300 times, we break the old habit and form a new one thus enabling us to perform the new habit unconsciously or effortlessly. I think that this discovery is a big deal. It proves that anyone can change, if willing.

It requires repeating the same steps over and over again while adding an increased measure of intensity. Increase the intensity of the act and you will create muscle memory while flexing your way into new strength and vitality to your efforts. Away with the old ways. Out the door with the stale and useless patterns. And forget about the former choices. Only the new patterns, new habits, new ways of thinking are valuable enough to exist in the new mental and lifestyle space that you are creating.

Take out the scaffold of discipline and get ready to balance each level with steady and grounded movement! When you are disciplined, you can achieve destiny and change. Discipline equals diligence and diligence determines reward. Nehemiah, a biblical leader, made an unprecedented mark on the society and history of his day. According to Smith's Bible Name Dictionary, he began his journey as a slave and cupbearer for a Persian king, King Artaxerxes Longimanus, before becoming the Governor of Judea and Repairer of the Jerusalem walls. His continual acts of discipline shifted Jerusalem from the ruins of a vagabond land to a regional force with economic, social, religious, and governmental power. One single act of courage pursued by many small disciplines led to one of the greatest measures of change in Jewish history.

Discipline impacts results. Nehemiah took on a major project to bring a tremendous measure of change to those for whom he cared most. His 'why' made the difference. The knowledge of why he did it suggests that discipline rooted in the love and care for others is most powerful. Since this is true, it supports my thoughts regarding the Greater Principle. The Greater Principle, as mentioned in chapter one, suggests that change is most conceivable when connected to a greater person or purpose. Discipline for the cause of self often becomes a powerless reasoning for change. Discipline for the cause and sake of others gives long-term life and destiny to a course of action.

The Why Factor

Determining your "why" to succeed, change, or grow is just as necessary as determining the process in which you engage to attain that success, change, or growth. The process of what I will call "why factor," is not some new concept. Simon Sinek popularized the concept with his book Start With Why. It is a proven discipline in the marketplace, personal development, entrepreneurship, and many other areas. It is as relevant to growing into your greatness as positive self-talk or servant leadership. Determining your why has been linked to massive achievement and extreme levels of peak performance and productivity. Your why is your reason for what you do and deploys your determination, resilience, and fight into action. Your why is at the core of your "grit." Grit has become a recent study in psychological fields. Psychologists are formulating studies to explain why individuals from extremely negative and challenging circumstances appear to outperform academically or professionally those from less challenging and even more structured environments. The results seem to center around grit. Grit then can be described as the internal dogmatic fight and will within an individual to achieve, soar, and succeed at their goals, dreams, and destiny.

What is your why? Do you have the grit to do whatever it takes, give up whatever is necessary, develop the discipline to win at change, success, and growth? If not, find the grit to do it. Look in the mirror, into your eyes, and demand grit from yourself. Walk away with the will, determination, and internal dogmatic fight to win. Be relentless! Take some time to list the desired goals, dreams, ambitions, and changes in your life followed by the "why" for those goals, dreams, changes, and ambitions.

Now ask yourself, "Is my why strong enough?" Is my why powerful enough to draw the tenacity to survive and succeed out of me?" You must be able to answer these questions with a definitive yes. If you don't possess a definitive yes, then develop a why that is strong enough. As long as it is authentic.

The road to greatness is pathed with obstacles and plenty of reasons to quit. If change, success, and growth were easy, everyone would win. Everyone would get a gold medal at the Olympic Games. There would be no need for a silver or bronze medal. Yet there is. Why? One person's "why" was greater than the others. The Olympic Gold Medalist was the true champion with the most grit. Where is your grit? Give all the grit you have into what you are attempting to achieve. Grit is gruesome, tiring, painful, ugly, and pricey but grit wins gold medals. Robert Kiyosaki, Author of Rich Dad Poor Dad, and Financial Advisor said, *"The size of your success is measured by the strength of your desire; the size of your dream; and how you manage disappointment along the way.* Do you want Gold, or would you just rather pacify yourself with Bronze? Come on. Be relentless! Sacrifice.

The unofficial definition of discipline is sacrifice. Sacrifice for love is the greatest sacrifice in existence. History records some of the greatest acts of humankind based on love. Can you recall a time or instance that you practiced self-discipline because you were doing it for someone or something greater than you? Something or someone that you loved. Maybe it was for your football team, band competition, retired parents, or even community. Reflect back on how much you invested into being disciplined enough to win, help out, or do your part. Was it amazing? Did you do things that you have never done? Were you not more alive than ever before? Yes, you were. I know you were. I know you were because I have had the same experiences.

Plan Well

Discipline requires planning, organizing, and prioritizing. In order to make planning, organizing, and prioritizing applicable, you must be willing to engage the three with the utmost intensity. Clinging to each with the grip of life or death will teach you the power and transformation. Each one has the power of both life and death for our transformation. What do I mean? Applying each appropriately, intensely, and intimately will build your dreams, inspire your creativity and ingenuity, as well as sail you into destiny. Avoid them and all of that which you could have will drown in the sea of passivity (lack of aggression or grit) in route to the island of Amazing Things. You choose. Planning, organizing, and prioritizing thrive in the soil of discipline. However, discipline needs a target. Lay out a plan that requires self-discipline. Discipline has to be aimed at something significant to change. Discipline must therefore be aimed at plans, strategies, and priorities. On a smaller scale discipline is aimed at daily goals, objectives, regimens, and routines that achieve plans, organization, and priorities. Daily discipline equates to daily success.

When small steps are overlooked, unappreciated, and seldom celebrated, big steps can appear to be too big to accomplish. Believe me, when you celebrate and build on the little steps, you maintain the fuel, focus, and fervor necessary to finish well.

I have learned to appreciate small steps because most times that is all I have achieved-small steps. Each small step was a success toward a big goal. In success psychology this is called the Law of Accumulation. The Law of Accumulation is a financial concept that is universal and transferable to any arena of life. Brian Tracy teaches that The Law of Accumulation suggests that *every great financial achievement is an accumulation of hundreds of small efforts and sacrifices that no one ever sees or appreciates.* I was forced to appreciate small success because of a lack of ability in me to be influential, network, relate, and steward my blessing. Furthermore, I understand that in every circumstance there is either a lesson to learn or a gift granted. God saw fit for me to learn more along the way. He will do the same for you!

The more you learn along the way, the hungrier you become for the vision, dream, business, degree, organization, etc. Small steps teach you to be humble and become interdependent with the rest of society. If not for the small steps forging a network, merger, or collaboration, most of us would suffer alone. The more disciplined we are with habits, gifts, anointing, talents, finances, etc., the more successful we become in life! Aristotle wrote, *"We are what we repeatedly do."* According to author Darren Hardy, in his book The Compound Effect, *"Psychological studies reveal that 95 percent of everything we feel, think, do, and achieve is a result of a learned habit."* He teaches that little steps of habit change compounded over time delivers astronomical results. Mastering habits, especially changing them, means jumping in with both feet and eyes wide open. It means being "fully present" in the process. Change your habits and you can change your life.

Chapter Conclusions

1. The Self-Discipline Principle suggests that mastering self-discipline in your life is necessary for fulfilling your goal and sustaining a focused path.

2. Tracy argues that self-discipline is the ability to do what you should do, when you should do it, whether you feel like it or not.

3. Napoleon Hill, author of the book Think and Grow Rich, which has sold over 15 million copies said, *"Self-discipline is the master key to riches."* Mastering your behavior is ultimately the key to successful change.

4. Determining your "why" to succeed, change, or grow is just as necessary as determining the process in which you engage to attain that success, change, or growth.

5. Grit has become a recent study in psychological fields. Psychologists are formulating studies to explain why individuals from extremely negative and challenging circumstances appear to outperform personally and professionally those from less challenging and even more structured environments. The results seem to center around grit. Grit then can be described as the internal dogmatic fight and will within an individual to achieve, soar, and succeed at their goals, dreams, and destiny.

6. Do you have the grit to do whatever it takes, give up whatever is necessary, develop the discipline to win at change, success, and growth? If not, find the grit for it. Look in the mirror, into your eyes, and demand the grit from yourself. Walk away with the will, determination, and internal dogmatic fight to win. Be relentless! Take some time to list the desired goals, dreams, ambitions, and changes in your life followed by the "why" for those goals, dreams, change, and ambitions.

7. Planning, organizing, and prioritizing thrive in the soil of discipline. However, discipline needs a target. Lay out a plan that requires self-discipline. Discipline has to be aimed at something significant to change. Discipline must then be aimed at plans, strategies, and priorities. Do it now. Be relentless!

Chapter 13

The Fully Present Principle

The Fully Present Principle suggests that in order to get the most out of any situation you must fully participate and be fully engaged.

At the caterpillar stage the egg eats, searches, and forms in an effort to transform through the next stage of growth. The next stage of growth is the Pupa Stage. Speaking of stages, do you happen to know your current stage of growth? What is the next stage of development, change, and growth for you? It is actually unnatural and unsuccessful for you to remain at the same skillset, mindset, and achievement for the rest of your life. Ask yourself the question and give a definitive answer, "What is next for me?" What do I see for sure on the horizon and landscape of my future, destiny, growth, change, and success? Just a glimpse of what is next will grant you a spark of motivation, endurance, and energy to fire up the chambers of your grit and will so that you leap far into the next stage. Can you do it? Do you believe that there is more or can be more for you? Can there be more joy, hope, peace, family, rest, vacation, leadership, friendship, opportunity, and growth at this juncture in your life? How would you know unless you shift out of pre-contemplation stage and through contemplation stage into action stage? I think it is time to evolve. Let's go. I am with you all the way. In the Pupa stage the caterpillar spins a silk web around itself, fastens down, and goes into metamorphosis. This means that the caterpillar is fully present in its transformation. It has eaten enough to grow. At this stage, we should do as the caterpillar-eat enough to grow.

The entire concept of "eating until you grow" is reflected in my personal practice of being a lifelong student. I have committed to learning and growing for the rest of my journey. I often hear it said that the mistake for those who graduate from college is that after graduation, they stop reading books, researching, and studying. Therefore, they dull the axe of knowledge and understanding. Change, success, and growth require continual learning for the rest of your life! Cordell Hull, Former Secretary of State and Nobel Peace Prize Winner said this of being a student, *"You are always a student, never a master. You have to keep moving forward."* If you recall, the word metamorphosis means "complete change." Our growth goal is complete change. The caterpillar begins to experience a complete change. At some point in our efforts to develop we have to shift from taking in the process to becoming one with the process. The nuance is instantaneous response rather than delayed reaction. In order to be fully present in our transformation we must shift from initial action to fully engaged action. Action is the next step of change after contemplation. Action should never stay the same. Action has to evolve, intensify, and scale.

Encased

The lesson for successful change is in the caterpillar metamorphose. We will continue using the caterpillar as a symbol of change. Like the caterpillar, we must become encased in our process of change. This is the only way of achieving optimal results. Remember that we are not working on a warped mutation that resembles growth but a genuine complete metamorphosis. Right? If so, we must be fully encased in the process. This means that there can be no room for distractions. The caterpillar gets completely encased within its' cocoon. Distractions are not a part of the plan. The transformation that you need for success, growth, and change requires the type of determination that does not allow distractions to alter the course. It requires isolation, encapsulation, and laser focus. Do you have it?

So, what is the idea of being "fully present"? How does it work? Are there real benefits if I thrust myself into the process? Let's explore this idea. First, I love the idea of being "fully present." I love it because I am a servant at heart. I love giving myself to whomever or whatever I am supporting. Contribution is one of my core values. So, learning and embracing the whole idea of "fully present" was an exhilarating and stimulating soul journey for me. I learned about the concept of being "fully present" during my post graduate studies in Organizational Leadership and Coaching at Regent University. As part of my educational tract, I was Certified and Credentialed as a Life and Professional Leadership Coach. I learned how to coach toward both personal and professional development goals from a biblical worldview. I loved it! My coaching coursework required countless hours and hands-on training in the concepts of effective coaching and the coaching methodology.

One of the concepts in particular was the practice of being "fully present" with clients in order to give the client one hundred percent of undisturbed, undistracted, unsolicited, emotionally intelligent attention. This means that the coach and the client were the only two people existing in the world during the coaching sessions. The discipline requires refraining from looking at your watch to check the time. It also requires refraining from thinking about your next appointment. Other components of the discipline are listening deeply, silencing the inner voice while the client is speaking, refusing to answer the phone, and reducing how often one writes while the client is talking. In addition, excellent eye contact is a must.

Can you get there with your process to change, growth, and success? Can you give the process one hundred percent of your undisturbed, undistracted, unsolicited, emotionally intelligent attention? In order to achieve this level of self-discipline one may have to deny time with friends, refrain from marking time, and choose not to obsess over what's next. Do you have grit? If so, identify your distractions and mutilate them. Totally obliterate them one hundred percent. Do not waste another breath dealing with distractions. Get to the business of focusing on what you need to do and when you need to do it. It is necessary for old habits and parts of your psychology to die off in order to make room for the new to sprout and spring forward.

Pruning

Did you know that removing forty percent of the peach tree each year causes new growth each spring? In agriculture this is known as pruning. Pruning is a process of removing unnecessary parts of something in order for it to experience healthier growth. Pruning doesn't just happen with plants. It also occurs with brain development. Psychologists refer to pruning as part of the process of shedding unnecessary neurons to improve overall brain function. Actually, the concept of removing the old for the new is quite universal. Jesus taught about spiritual pruning. In John 15:1-2, Jesus says, *"I am the true vine, and my Father is the gardener. He cuts off every branch in me that bears no fruit, while every branch that does bear fruit he prunes so that it will be even more fruitful."* (NIV) The Greek word for prunes also means cleans. In the case of Jesus' teaching, God cleans His children of unrighteous deeds, habits, and thoughts so that more spiritual ones grow. So, life proceeds death. Something must die in order for something better to live.

The caterpillar experiences death and life simultaneously. It is not that the caterpillar is fully dead in the cocoon process. Parts of it die and parts of it continue to live. Cells are broken down and rebuilt inside the cocoon. It develops new parts in preparation for destiny, success, change, and growth. Our human eyes only get the opportunity to see the final product. Yet, the change is happening inside before it is seen outside. The old form, habits, and survival strategies of the caterpillar pass on to the grave of yesterday while the new form, habits, and survival strategies are sprouting forth in preparation for tomorrow. Like the butterfly, we must experience a pruning process to become the best version of ourselves. Soaring into our destined purpose calls for the removal of what is unnecessary for the next level or dimension of greatness. In life, growth can require relocation from one geography to the next, losing one relationship for another, and experiencing hardship that bring out the best in us.

The Apostle Paul wrote in Romans 12:2, *"Do not conform to the pattern of this world but be transformed by the renewing of your mind. Then you will be able to test and approve what God's will is—his good, pleasing, and perfect will."* (NIV) In this passage the original Greek word for transformed is metamorphose meaning completely changed. It signifies an outward display of what first changed inwardly. Your life strategy for change has to be like that of the caterpillar if you are going to completely change. The old form, habits, and survival strategies must pass on to the grave of yesterday while the new form, habits, and survival strategies sprout forth in preparation for tomorrow. As a matter of fact, it's normal for parts of you to die. What is new is well worth the funeral of what is old. Many people are afraid of letting go. Some are mentally and emotionally diseased by holding on to old, useless things and perpetually memorializing them. They are called hoarders. It is an awful disease where people live with things of far-gone value for the rest of their lives.

They carry along the worthless baggage and memories of the past. This leaves them weighed down and clogged with lifeless stuff. Look for signs of memorialization. What are you memorializing within your habits, lifestyle, surroundings, etc. that may need a eulogy and a proper burial? Do not waste time! Act now. You will not be left empty-handed. Something useful will grow in its place if you allow it.

New Things

Change, success and growth require new habits for attaining destiny, purpose, and dream fulfillment. Trees give us an ideal symbolism and great characteristics of change development. Before I gained insight into why trees are so barren during the dry, cold winter season, I used to feel so sorry for barren looking trees. It is humorous but true. I used to think, *"Oh that poor tree. It was once beautiful with leaves. Now look at it. It is all puny and dull."* I would really become saddened for the tree.

One day I was faced with the task of eulogizing a very dear friend. His life was a tragic loss. At the time, he was one of the few people that I could count on one hand as a friend. I loved him like a brother. He was working so hard at change, but the pressure of life was too much for him. His perspective of his situation was faulty, and he felt compelled to take his life. He left behind two children and a young struggling wife as well as a friend struggling to comfort his family at his passing when the friend needed comforting himself. Of course, the friend in this story is me.

The fall season was passing, and winter was approaching quickly. After gathering myself to preach his eulogy, I traveled to the city where the funeral was held. As we drew near to the church, I saw a vast area of barren trees. As I began feeling sorry for the trees, which was my usual custom, I suddenly felt the urge to research why trees have no leaves in the winter. I grabbed my smart phone and quickly googled the topic "why trees lose their leaves in the winter." Much to my surprise I discovered that trees do not lose their leaves, but they intentionally shed them for survival.

I found that trees nourish the branches and leaves from water that is pulled through the roots and transferred to the rest of the tree parts.

During the fall and winter, which are the dry seasons, trees tend to reserve water and cut off the canal to the limbs and leaves in order to have enough water in the rest of the tree to survive the dry spell. Smart tree wouldn't you say? My discovery was that the tree forces the leaves to die to preserve life and growth. Because of the ecological process, new leaves will grow in place of the old. I soon realized why I was compelled to learn the lesson about the tree on that particular day and during that season of grief in my life. I needed to know that although some things and people die, life brings new relationships and opportunities in place of what was lost. I used the lesson that I had learned about the barren tree to bring hope to my good friend's family in their time of loss. I actually incorporated the lesson into my sermon. You too can learn the lesson of the tree. Letting go can be complicated, intimidating, and uncertain; however, it is possible.

If you can do it, you can possess a greater start. I recall a Scripture from a book of Job. Job is about an honest, giving, and just man who undeservingly lost everything in a short period of time. Job lost his wealth, children, health, and influence. Yes, he lost everything except his faith. Yet, in the process he held on to the hope of a new start. Along his journey, Job experienced times of grief and wonder.

These occasions led to some of the most profound teachings and concepts. Consider this one about the tree. Job 14:7-9 says, *"For there is hope for a tree, if it is cut down, that it will sprout again, and that its tender shoots will not cease. Though its root may grow old in the earth, and its stump may die in the ground, yet at the scent of water it will bud and bring forth branches like a plant."* (NKJV) Is not that a beautiful thing? So is the beauty of your new start. Job ultimately learned that he could have a beautiful new start as well. Know that you can let go of habits, people, substances, and other things while making room for the new. The process begins inside.

Chapter Conclusions

1. The Fully Present Principle suggests that in order to get the most out of any situation you must fully participate and be fully engaged.

2. It is actually unnatural and unsuccessful for you to remain at the same skillset, mindset, and achievement for the rest of your life. Ask yourself the question and give a definitive answer, "What is next for me?" What do I see for sure on the horizon and landscape of my future, destiny, growth, change, and success?

3. You should never stop learning. I often hear it said that the mistake for those who graduate from college is that after graduation, they stop reading books, researching, and studying. Therefore, they dullen the axe of knowledge and understanding ultimately failing to be a student for life.

4. The transformation that you need for success, growth, and change must be a focused, peaceful, and undisturbed process. It requires a slight measure of isolation, intense concentration, and laser focus. Is the value of your change, success, and growth greater than the pain of the process to get there? Do you have grit?

5. Your life strategy for change has to be like that of the caterpillar if you are going to completely change. The old form, habits, and survival strategies must pass on to the grave of yesterday while the new form, habits, and survival strategies sprout forth in preparation for tomorrow. It is normal for parts of you to die.

6. What are you memorializing within your habits, lifestyle, surroundings, etc. that may need a eulogy and a proper burial? Do not waste time. Act now. You will not be left empty-handed. Something useful will grow in its place if you allow it.

7. Know that you can let go of habits, people, substances, and other things while making room for the new. The process begins inside.

*The whole point of being alive is to **evolve into the complete person** you were intended to be.*

- Oprah Winfrey, Talk Show Host and Author

If you paint in your mind a picture of bright and happy expectations, you put yourself into a condition conducive to your goals.

-Norman Vincent Peale, Author, and Theologian

Chapter 14

The Inside/Out Principle

The Inside/Out Principle suggests that all significant change happens on the inside first then becomes visible on the outside.

When a seed is planted underground, it takes some time before a farmer can tell that it is growing. If it were not for the knowledge of the inside/out principle, the farmer could possibly give up on the seed. However, what the farmer knows is that the seed, though underground, is *germinating*. When a seed is germinating, it nourishes off the nutrients of the soil. It grows underneath the soil from the inside out. What is inside bursts through the seed shell breaking through the surface of the ground and springs upward to the outside world. Therefore, the growth that was happening all along on the inside, though unseen, shows up on the outside. The process for the caterpillar's transformation into a beautiful, dazzling butterfly has similarities to that of a plant seed. Once the caterpillar cocoons itself, all of the work is happening on the inside. Real change happens inside before the evidence of it shows up on the outside. Such is the process for you and I. The development of any new habit, skill, change, etc. begins within you and later materializes into the world of your circumstances, goals, dreams, and success. The critical key is practicing patience in the process. Patience is tremendously rewarding, but extremely hard to master. Why? Our soul wants what it wants when it wants it. A hungry soul can be utterly hard to discipline. However, practice increases the power of discipline. So, practice often.

Progress Has A Process

Progress does not usually happen instantaneously; but it happens rather slowly. Although progress most often happens slowly, when we are consistent in the end we attain the prize. Progress for the caterpillar to transform into a beautiful, dazzling butterfly is slow just like most change, success, and growth. As a matter of fact, there are not very many overnight wonders of which I am familiar. Daniel Gilbert, Harvard psychologist and author of Stumbling on Happiness, says that if we gave lottery losers each thirty seconds on TV to announce that they lost, it would take nine years to get through the losers of a single drawing. Gilberts' discovery is dated. The present numbers would surely have increased by now. Even with winning the lotto, most people play it over and over again before winning any significant amount of money. By the way, did you know that instant success often leads to failure and unhealthy living? I recently read an article which suggested that most people who win millions of dollars in the lottery ultimately end up broke in a matter of a few years. How does one end up broke in just a few years after winning millions? I will tell you how.

The winners did not pay the painstaking price of blood, sweat, and tears for what they won. Therefore, they failed to respect, honor, and appreciate the wealth once they received it. Furthermore, the process of obtaining wealth came without any training or self-discipline. In other words, nothing about it was transformative. Nothing about the process changed them or made them better people. Someone once said, *"Money only brings out of you more of that which is already in you."* If this is true, if you are a poor steward before the wealth, you are likely to be one afterwards.

I have often heard it said that patience is a virtue. Virtues are good qualities. When someone says that you have virtue or you display virtuous character traits, that is a compliment. Patience is a good quality to possess. It is required to achieve any real measure of success, growth, and change. A caterpillar does not become a butterfly overnight. Destiny, success, achievement, prosperity, inventions, and the like do not usually happen overnight. It shows up a little at a time. However, a genius plan for coping with the sometimes overwhelming, slow pace of change, growth, and success is to practice what is called reinforcement management. Another coping process is self-liberation. Let's begin by identifying what is reinforcement management. Reinforcement management can be addressed with punishment or reward. There is good common ground for both. Some people will deny themselves something that they really want if they fail at the goal which is punishment reinforcement management. Others will reward themselves with something that they really want if they achieve the goal, change, or success which is reward reinforcement management. The choice of which to use depends on what works best for the individual. Others practice a combination of both. Nevertheless, reinforcement management is a way to stay on track to achievement when you are running out of willpower, determination, grit, or whatever and are ready to throw in the towel.

Identify which process works best for you. Maybe it is a combination of both. In my Insane Productivity training with Darren Hardy, he mentioned the application of punishment over the application of reward. He has found that punishment seems to have a weightier threat and impact than reward. It seemed to have worked wonders for his audience base and maybe it will also work for you. I am not quite at the punishment reinforcement management level yet. I choose reward. I am easy. You can enlist friends, relatives, trainers, etc. to help you achieve the change, goal, dream, or success desired. So, what is self-liberation? Self-liberation is both belief and commitment that one can change. How well are you doing with self-liberation? Do you have the belief and the commitment to change? Belief is key to achieving the desired results. Consider the wisdom of Proverbs 23:7 which says, "For as he thinks within himself, so he is." (NASB)

Most Success Mentors, Coaches, Trainers, Religious Leaders, and Psychologists suggest positive self-talk as a means of personal empowerment. It is one of my focal points when mentoring aspiring leaders. It is the key to rewriting our internal story. Many people practice self-talk. However, it is mostly negative utterances of what we cannot do, how fearful we are to try, and what we do not believe. It is important to reverse that tone and rewrite that narrative. It will work wonders for you. For Nathaniel Branden, author of the book Six Pillars of Self-Esteem, self-affirmation or self-talk is the foundation for self-esteem. Branden identifies self-affirmation as an attitude. Self-talk is an extremely powerful tool of change, success, and growth. Declare to yourself today, "I can do this." You are on your way to the finished product. Remember Philippians 4:13 which says, "I can do all things through Him who strengthens me." (NASB) When stating Philippians encouragement does not work. You can always cry out to God. He will answer. Job said of Him, "I know that You can do all things. And that no plan is impossible for You." (NASB) God has your back. Now, get to it! Start some positive self-talk, self-liberation, and reinforcement management. What's next for you is greater than what's behind you.

Better Days Ahead

What does the finished product of your change, growth, destiny, dreams, and success look like in your mind's eye? The necessity of this one warrants our attention. It is imperative that you possess the vision of it and hold on for dear life. You must remember that after all of the pain, change, self-discipline, courage, blood, sweat, and tears required to get to the final image, destiny and success are worth the work. Having this image in your mind, on paper, written in your vision statement, or in your strategic plan will always give you something to refer back to in challenging times. The final product for the butterfly is far greater than its beginning. Such is the process for us. Our destination, purpose, greatness, success, and dreams are far greater than where we start. Furthermore, the journey prunes us into maturity so that we possess the character to remain once we take the final form.

I am reminded of what Jim Rohn and Chris Widener wrote about development in the process of pursuing your dream in their book Twelve Pillars. Michael, the primary young character in the book, was mentored by Mr. Davis. Micheal sought Mr. Davis's wisdom on becoming wealthy. In one of their many intimate conversations about life, Mr. Davis asked Michael why he wanted money. Michael went on to mention the visible signs of Mr. Davis's vast wealth such as his house, cars, etc. Mr. Davis responded to Michael, *"After you become a millionaire, you can give it all away because what's important is not the million dollars. What's important is the person you have to become in the process of becoming a millionaire."* Our better days are on the other side and in the hands of the better person that we become throughout the journey. Life requires wise stewardship so that frail humanity can make decisions that change the world. Refuse to find greater value in materialism than you do in humanitarianism. Our greatness is a gift to the world around us not just the world we create around us. The key is to consistently work on self regardless of how long it takes.

Hang in There

During metamorphosis, the caterpillar, encased in the cocoon, chooses to either hang headfirst or legs first from a stable place until it's fully transformed into a butterfly. The success is in its ability to hang there for duration of the appointed time. All developments have a time and season. Especially development, change, and transformation in the hands of God. At the appointed time and season in the change process, the butterfly breaks forth into the dawn of a new day. So will you if you hang in there like the butterfly. Every process has its season. The concept of appointed time is clear in the biblical narrative of Abraham and Sarah's. Abraham and Sarah believed and were trying to have a child but could not because of Sarah's condition. Because God had a plan for Abraham's greatness, He sent divine men to Abraham to inform him that Sarah would soon conceive. When the divine men spoke to Abraham about Sarah's conception they said, *"Is anything too hard for the Lord? I will return to you at the appointed time next year, and Sarah will have a son."* (Genesis 18:14, NIV)

Everything has a time and place. While facing a difficult change in my life that seemed to last an eternity, I sought the Bible for hope and inspiration. I heard about its insight, wisdom, and moral guidance to truth. While doing research on timing and seasons, I discovered a scripture that gave me hope. Located in the Old Testament book Ecclesiastes 3:1, written by King Solomon, one of the sons of King David, is written, *"There is a season (a time appointed) for everything and a time for every delight and event or purpose under heaven."* (Amplified Bible) If you hang in there, your change, success, and growth must climax into destiny, opportunity, and goal achievement.

In our last stage of change, we discussed the Inside Out Principle. At this stage of change, we enter into "action-mode." We are working, avoiding, evolving, and fully participating; however, we are at our greatest vulnerability. We are more sensitive at this stage of the process which means that we could relapse and perish. Choosing to entertain the wrong thoughts, partake of toxins, or fail to avoid a predator means the end. For the butterfly this is the Pupa stage where it is fully wrapped in its cocoon developing and shaping for destiny. Like the caterpillar, when we are shaping and developing for destiny it is necessary to be observant to stay motivated.

Change is oftentimes more *"other-initiated"* than *"self-initiated."* Think about it. When was the last time you self-initiated a major uprooting or overhaul in your life? Some would say, "A long time ago." Others will say, "Never." Now compare that thought to the last time your circumstances forced you to change, overhaul or uproot and start over. Like most people, you have experienced more forced change than self-initiated change. It is often a bi-product and response to our external environment rather than our internal drive to get better, more skilled, or advance into our best self. Once we have gone through our major formative stages in anything we do, we plateau. We level out and develop a system of comfort and control. It is second nature for us to fall back into what is manageable rather than what is challenging. Therefore, we have to continually monitor if we have begun to lose heart for what is greater ahead for what is comfortable and stable now. There is stability in change; however, before stability comes growth. Hang in there and be observant. You may overlook the small things.

Chapter Conclusions

1. The Inside/Out Principle suggests that all significant change happens on the inside first then becomes visible on the outside.

2. When a seed is planted underground it takes some time before a farmer can tell that it is growing. If it were not for the knowledge of the inside/out principle, the farmer could possibly give up on the seed. Real change happens inside before the evidence of it shows up on the outside.

3. Progress does not usually happen instantaneously, but it happens rather slowly. The caterpillar's transformation into a beautiful, dazzling butterfly is a slow progression. There are not very many overnight wonders of which I am familiar.

4. Self-liberation is both belief and commitment that you can change. How well are you doing with self-liberation? Do you have the belief and the commitment? Do you have belief but no commitment? Try self-talk. Self-talk is a proven and successful method of success, change, growth, achievement, etc. Most Success Mentors, Coaches, Trainers, Religious Leaders, and Psychologists suggest positive self-talk as a means of personal empowerment.

5. What does the finished product of your change, growth, destiny, dreams, and success look like in your mind's eye? It is imperative that you possess the vision of it and hold on for dear life. You must remember that after all of the pain, change, self-discipline, courage, blood, sweat, and tears required to get to the final image, destiny and success are worth the work.

6. All things have a time and season. At the appointed time and season in the change process, the butterfly breaks forth into the dawn of a new day. So, will you if you hang in there like the butterfly. Hard times, difficulties, challenges, and change often create the disillusion that life will "always be this way."

7. There is stability in change; however, before stability comes growth. Hang in there and be observant; you may overlook the small things. You know that they are important too. Right?

Your decisions shape your destiny. The future is what you make of it. Little, everyday decisions will either take you to the life you desire or to disaster by default.

-Anthony Robbins, Entrepreneur and Author

It's the little details that are vital. Little things make big things happen.

-John Wooden, Basketball Hall of Fame Coach and Player

Chapter 15

The Observation Principle

The Observation Principle suggests that it is a necessity to recognize and acknowledge the success of your development.

Like a mother in the final trimester of pregnancy, you have to be sensitive to everything that is taking place inside of and around you during your development. Birthing change is similar to birthing life. It is actually identical in some respects. A new you forms out of the process of change. Once the new you forms, the old you no longer exists. The Old Testament Prophet Isaiah, speaking for God to Israel, said, *"Do not remember the former things, nor consider the things of old. Behold, I will do a new thing. Now it shall spring forth. Shall you not know it? I will even make a road in the wilderness and rivers in the desert.* (Isaiah 43:18-19, NKJV) Behold means to see or observe. Here is where observation balances motivation. At some point the progress of change shifts from indirect and small to direct and significantly noticeable. When I can see the change that I can be, it motivates me. When you see the change that you can be, it will motivate you. Observation ties effort to vision. It is the light that fuels the fire of willpower and belief to achieve the goal ahead. You have to notice and distinctively mark small successes. The more you do this, the more the reality in which you will finish sets.

Great Observation

We often stop to cheer ourselves on. Great still, there is a growing need for us to practice healthy celebration. Practicing celebration supports great self-care and mental health. Consider the drama and challenges that accompany other-initiated change, practicing celebration improved morality and self-image. Therefore, it is beneficial to mark the ways in which you are transforming into your best self. Identify how well you are flexing your muscles of adaptability. Observing how well you are doing is invaluable information towards finishing the process. Observation is about seeing!

The challenge some have with seeing is that seeing they see not. In other words, change can be taking place around them, yet they lack the attention to see it. Thus, they fail to observe it. Sometimes growth can be so microscopic that life's distractions lure us away from attentiveness. The difference between seeing and observing is attention. Observing means to pay attention while making mental notes or even establishing a written record. Because some fail to pay attention and give mental notes or record, they miss the boat of opportunity floating upstream to their destiny. Others can be so bent on the past or the way things used to be that they cannot release the things of old. Avoid both! Remember, you are not in this process alone. God is with you. He is often creating new things in and around you.

There are six signs to practicing great observational skills. These six signs give clear internal confirmation that you possess what it takes to notice and celebrate small transformation. Good observers pay attention, make mental notes, form connections, meditate regularly, eliminate distractions, and memorize.

When any combination of these confirmation as settling within us, we have become serious. We are in tune with what we want and where we are going. We acknowledge that we have developed what the old folk call a "deaf ear" toward anything contrary to our destiny. When we arrive here, we are laser focused. We become so zoomed in on one specific thing that any slight adjustment sets off alarms that something is off track. Can you do that for yourself, your goals, your dreams, your change, and your success? Can you lock in and function in the six internal signs of a good observer?

Best Effort

Whatever the cause is for your change, growth, or success, give it your absolute best and most concentrated effort. Be like the Eagle that can see the prey two miles away. Be the Tarsier that can see in the darkness of the night as if it was daylight. Be like the Chameleon that can have both eyes look in opposite 180-degree directions at the same time noticing both predator and prey. Come on. You can do this. For this one chapter of your life give destiny your absolute all. Sometimes we are too timid and afraid to practice our best effort. However, the best way to succeed is to be willing to fail. Risk whatever it takes within reason to become the person you are destined to be. You must overcome every challenge for your change. Great success requires great concentration. What is concentration? We can examine it from the minds of people who could not have achieved success without it. Athletics is an arena that requires a great deal of concentration.

Serena Williams, Tiger Woods, Micheal Jordan, and others forced themselves to achieve greatness, change, success, and purpose through unwavering concentration at each stage of their journey and development. Serena Williams, #1 Ranking American Tennis Player, said of concentration, *"If you can keep playing tennis when somebody is shooting a gun down the street, that's concentration."* Serena did not ascend to her number one status by default, luck, or lack of grit. She mustered up the concentration required to achieve the goal. Arnold Palmer is one of the greatest Professional Golfers of all times. His legacy is so historical that you can go into many restaurants today, sit down for an ice-cold glass of sweet tea, and if you add lemonade to it, the server may just call your drink by his name, Arnold Palmer. When we are drinking half tea and half lemonade we're drinking an Arnold Palmer. When asked to clarify his definition of concentration, Arnold Palmer said, *"What do I mean by concentration? I mean focusing totally on the business at hand and commanding your body to do exactly what you want it to do."* Best efforts requires the bravery to command yourself rather than comfort yourself.

Arnold has figured out something very significant. Concentration has to be commanded not motioned, asked, or negotiated, but commanded. Command concentration and you will achieve. Charles Ray "Chuck" Norris, Martial Artist, Actor, and Producer has left his mark in American entertainment and sports. I watched lots of Chuck Norris karate growing up. I was a bit of a Chuck Norris imitator, including wearing the headband. In his own words, Chuck was not the ideal candidate for athleticism.

However, he practiced such a high level of daily concentration that he excelled above anyone in his sport. When describing how concentration changed his life, Chuck said, *"Whatever luck I had, I made. I was never a natural athlete, but I paid my dues in sweat and concentration and took the time necessary to learn karate and become a world champion."* Chuck takes the guesswork out of defining concentration. Concentration then is the dues we pay for success, change, destiny, and growth. Concentrate rigorously and you will excel to the highest pinnacle of mental toughness. Then, your mind will complement your mission.

Chapter Conclusions

1. The Observation Principle suggests that it is a necessity to recognize and acknowledge the success of your development.

2. Like a mother in the final trimester of pregnancy, you have to be sensitive to everything that is taking place inside of and around you during your development.

3. Observation is about seeing! The challenge some have with seeing is that seeing they see not. In other words, change can be taking place around them, yet they lack the attention to see it. As a result, they fail to observe it. The difference between seeing and observing is attention.

4. These six signs give clear internal signals that you possess what it takes to notice and celebrate all the small transformation towards your change, success, and growth. Good observers pay attention, make mental notes, form connections, meditate regularly, eliminate distractions, and memorize.

5. Whatever the cause is for your change, growth, or success, give it your absolute best and most concentrated effort. Be like the Eagle that can see the prey two miles away. Be the Tarsier that can see in the darkness of the night as if it was daylight. Be like the Chameleon that can have both eyes look in opposite 180-degree directions at the same time thus noticing both predator and prey.

6. Concentration has to be commanded not motioned, asked, or negotiated, but commanded. Command concentration and you will achieve.

7. Concentration then is the dues we pay for success, change, destiny, and growth. Concentrate and you will excel.

All our dreams can come true if we have the courage to pursue them.

-Walt Disney, Entrepreneur, Animator, and Producer

Just when the caterpillar thought the world was ending, he turned into a butterfly.

-Proverb

Chapter 16

The Completion Principle

The Completion Principle suggests that you can and will finish a destiny that you commit to until the end.

The Completion Principle is what I call the happy principle. Its' the happy principle because it opens mental doors that are locked toward actually achieving the goal. It slings wide the doors of possibility. We often war with mental barriers deep within the corridors of our belief system. These mental barriers create doubt, insecurity, and more. They are often embedded into our thought life through various seeds of trauma. However, the Completion Principles is in place to reassure that self-limiting beliefs do not prevail. We can arrive at our destiny and purpose regardless of the culture around us. I love this principle because it breathes hope. Hope is something that I believe so many people lack today. People remain in the same debilitating conditions, lifestyle, and mindsets because of a lack of hope. I learned the emotional benefits of hope through Proverbs 13:12 which says, *"Hope deferred makes the heart sick, but a longing fulfilled is a tree of life."* (NIV) There is a shortage of hope in our society, the next generation, and the way it looks, the future of our world. We live in the most lucrative, opportunistic era of time on the planet, yet too many people fail at hope. I have been in situations where I was shunned for being a dreamer, a hoper, a believer. After some time, I began to buy into the idea that something was wrong with me. As my knowledge of world affairs and global cultures grew, I realized that there was and is nothing wrong with hoping and dreaming. I wasn't the problem. I understood the hope is a tree of life.

For the caterpillar transformation is organic. It is a natural part of its biology. As it is for the butterfly, so it is for you and me. Change is a response to our biology. We naturally change with age, time, and circumstance. Therefore, we can trust in our autonomy. We grow because we have to and need it. All change is not organic, yet we can develop a naturally healthy response to change that is significant in our lives. The principle of completion proves that the caterpillar transforms into an adult butterfly. Adulthood is the final stage of the caterpillars' change. Adulthood confirms with evidence that the caterpillar has fully matured. It has arrived at destiny and purpose. The principle of completion establishes that like the butterfly we will arrive at our destiny and purpose. This means that when change is processed properly, we can mature into it. Destiny is the full maturity of your spiritual, personal, and professional development. The principle of completion reveals that we *become* the destiny more so than derive at the destination. We become the full embodiment of that in which we set forth to obtain.

Maturity is not instantaneous but methodological. It happens in stages, phases, up and downs, seasons and times, months and years, and decades and centuries. Change hardly ever happens fast, but often happens slower than we would like. Nevertheless, the end justifies the means. The prize is worth the process. The finish is worth the formula. The outcome is worth the output. Wealth is worth the work. The level is worth the legwork and the dimension is worth the development. These are benefits that yield great dividends for the next journey of development.

Benefits of Finishing

Change often rewards greater vision, value, and voice. Vision is about the ideal future that lies ahead. Value is about the worth, legacy, and acceptance we gain along the way. Voice is about influence, impact, and engagement toward the world around us. The caterpillar once matured into a butterfly benefit from the most formative dimension of vision, value, and voice. When we give in to our transformation process, we experience its' benefits. The benefits for the butterfly are that it goes from walking to flying. It also benefits from a greater level of beauty and function. Destiny allows the butterfly to reproduce itself. The caterpillar therefore became a contributing butterfly to the expansion and extension of its species. It can duplicate and multiply itself over and over thus adding value to its population.

Like the caterpillar, when you finish your transformation and destiny, you will be uniquely different. You will benefit in ways uniquely different from past times and stages in your life. Your life will literally be as different as the night is from the day. Places to which you had to metaphorically crawl, will become places in which you are able to metaphorically fly. Like the butterfly, your beauty and function peaks at the highest levels. Your associations will improve. Your influence will grow. Your impact will increase. Your reach will be unlimited at your level of access. Like the caterpillar turned butterfly, your vision will go to a much higher level. You will see at the butterfly level what you could never see at the caterpillar level. This means that the negative, intimidating, poisonous, predatory things that you used to see you will see no more. Erased. Gone. Toast. Zapped. Obliterated. You will be too high up for those low-level threats from your past to reach you. There are benefits waiting for you when you finish. And you will finish. I know that you will. I believe that by reading this book and making it to this chapter, you will finish and finish well. Remember that you must keep your mind sharp by being a life-long learner. You must stay focused and engaged. You must cocoon yourself into the process. You must hang in there. The outcome of your change is going to be unimaginable. You are going to look around and say, "Wow, how did I get here?" The history of your journey will multiply your value.

The Currency of Value

Your value will increase to an exponentially new range. There will be a change in your beauty and function. You will become a producer like the caterpillar turned butterfly. At the finish stage, you will be able to pour into the next generation of caterpillars. You will be able to exemplify willpower, reinforcement management, positive self-talk, vision, and observance that came from your personal process. Value is everything. Albert Einstein, Physicist and Nobel Peace Prize Winner said, *"Try not to become a person of success, but rather try to become a person of value."* All of life is adding or taking away value from the environment you have been given. The more value that we add to the generations behind us the more we contribute to repopulating greatness in the world.

You will duplicate and multiply yourself over and over again, thus adding value to society. Value speaks of worth, legacy, and acceptance. There are certain circles that are unobtainable without a specific measure of value. When you finish, your measure of value will gain you access into doors that were once shut off to you. More knowledge, improved skills, peak performance, changed habits, etc. always increase value. The caterpillar can now leave a legacy as a butterfly and as a finisher. As a butterfly, it now has legacy. As a caterpillar it had opportunity but as a butterfly legacy. You do not see many preserved caterpillars, but you do see preserved butterflies-that is legacy. Your legacy will be preserved when you finish. If you do not finish for any other reason, finish for your legacy.

This stage becomes relatively exciting for those who are Christians. The Christian belief system is that our God has His loving presence engaged in the process of our development. In other words, God is helping us along the way. In one instance, the Apostle Paul told the Christians at Philippi, *"For it is God who works in you both to will and to do for His good pleasure."* (Phil. 2:13, NKJV) He gives us strength where we are weak and grace where we fail. Because of this, there is certainty of change for Christians. Our destiny is secured in becoming who we are predestined to become and achieve. All of which is encased in being made in the image of Jesus Christ. Hebrews 12:2 says, *"Therefore we also, since we are surrounded by so great a cloud of witnesses, let us lay aside every weight, and the sin which so easily ensnares us, and let us run with endurance the race that is set before us, 2 looking unto Jesus, the [a]author and [b]finisher of our faith, who for the joy that was set before Him endured the cross, despising the shame, and has sat down at the right hand of the throne of God."* (NKJV)

The Bible says that the Lord is the author and finisher of the Christian faith. If you are not Christian, choose Jesus Christ today as your Lord and Savior. His sacrifice for our sins makes Him the author and finisher of our faith. Jesus finished. After His resurrection from the dead, He ascended into Heaven. He is not seated at the right hand of the Father with all power. He embodied the Completion Principle. Life is not complete with Jesus, and neither is transformation for destiny. Accepting Jesus is not about perfection or living a sinless life. It's about eternal life. It's about becoming children of The Most High God. It's about receiving eternal peace with the Father and rewards of the Abrahamic Covenant. We all relapse at time to our past ways, but choosing Jesus guarantees us the grace of reconciliation through His blood and the forgiveness of sin.

Chapter Conclusions

1. The Completion Principle suggests that you can and will finish a destiny that you commit to until the end.

2. The Completion Principle is what I call the happy principle. Its' the happy principle because it opens mental doors that are locked toward actually achieving the goal. It slings wide the doors of possibility.

3. Change often rewards greater vision, value, and voice. Vision is about the ideal future that lies ahead. Value is about the worth, legacy, and acceptance we gain along the way. Voice is about influence, impact, and engagement toward the world around us.

4. Change hardly ever happens fast, yet most always happens slower than we would like. Nevertheless, the end justifies the means. The prize is worth the process. The finish is worth the formula. The outcome is worth the output. Wealth is worth the work. The level is worth the legwork and the dimension is worth the development. The reward is life changing.

5. Like the caterpillar, when you finish at achieving change, growth, success, and destiny, you will be uniquely different. You will benefit in ways uniquely different from past times and stages in your life. Your life will literally be as different as the night is from the day. Places to which you had to "crawl," will now be places to which you are able to "fly."

6. At the finish stage, you will be able to pour into the next generation of caterpillars. You will be able to exemplify willpower, reinforcement management, positive self-talk, vision, and observance that came from your personal process. Value is everything. Albert Einstein, Physicist and Nobel Peace Prize Winner said, "Try not to become a person of success, but rather try to become a person of value."

7. Your legacy will be preserved when you finish. If you do not finish for any other reason, finish for your legacy.

Rather than viewing a brief relapse back to inactivity as a failure, treat it as a challenge and try to get back on track as soon as possible.
-Jimmy Connors, Former Champion Tennis Player

Failures, repeated failures, are finger posts on the road to achievement. One fails forward toward success.
-C. S. Lewis, British Novelist and Author

Chapter 17

The Relapse Principle

The Relapse Principle says that the potential to return to former stages of behavior is a real threat.

Winning and success are never easy. They always come with mental and physical challenges. These challenges can often create mental and psychological duress which often leads to feeling overwhelmed. Have you ever been there? I have. It is no fun. Most of us have vices that we run to. We shelter ourselves in hiding when are totally overwhelmed with life and responsibility. Although life requires maturity in every area, maturity is demanding. The demands of meeting all of our goals and expectations can leave us vulnerable and depleted. Because no one is perfect, the potential for relapse is a real threat. The reality of relapse should be understood. Relapse most often happens at the action-stage of change and transformation.

Remember, the action stage is when we are most vulnerable. It is when we are closest to change and breakthrough. Surely, there are certain changes from which we can never relapse. A caterpillar can never relapse to the egg stage. The adult butterfly can never relapse back to a Pupa. Once a person reaches adult age, he or she can never physically relapse to a teenager. It is impossible for some physical relapse to happen. *What is possible however is mental and behavioral relapse.* In other words, we can relapse back to some form of habit or way of thinking that we once possessed. This kind of relapse is most dangerous because we hide it well. It can go undetected for years by those around us. Therefore, our imposter syndrome creates a facade that keeps us help deficient. We become hostage to a mask marauder that we worked so hard to avoid. If gone unchecked for extensive periods of time, the greater enemy shifts from the one without to the one within.

We have noted that relapse occurs through depleted willpower. Willpower is not the only area of depletion that opens us up to relapse. Spiritual depletion is often at the top of the list. When our soul lacks the wisdom, revelation, guidance, and power of God, we are but mere mortals unequipped for enemy assault. *Relapse begins in our mind or within your thoughts.* The simple act of thinking, pondering, and meditating on the wrong action or behavior too long will birth and constitute fulfillment of the thought. Someone once said, *"All action is first conceived in the mind."* Once we believe it, we act on it almost subconsciously. What roots or plants in our subconscious often plays out in our lives. Think of the relapses that you have probably experienced. You will agree that the conception of it first came as an idea in your mind. Once you entertained the idea long enough, it conceived and birthed the habit that you worked so hard to avoid.

It is like a person's addiction to sugar which as you probably know is a large percentage of us. When a sugar addict has successfully purged and detoxed from cakes, sweets, sodas, and the like, they know better than to go on an eating spree cramming junk food down their throats.

The results would be a traumatic relapse. They cannot spend time watching all kinds of baking channels and reading numerous dessert cookbooks. They cannot sit around meditating on cakes and pies or else they will fulfill those thoughts. The wisdom found in Proverbs 23:7 says, *"For as he thinks in his heart, so is he in behavior – one who manipulates."* (Amplified Bible) The key to success is in training your mind to think towards what changes you instead of what chains you.

Relapse Forward

The term relapse is so synonymous with drug or alcohol addiction that it's scarcely used in another context. However, we will apply it here for deeper consideration. A person can arguably relapse back into any state or stage. It's no secret that we all periodically fall back into an old way of thinking or being. This is the very essence of a relapse. However, like failing forward, we can relapse forward. Failing forward is simply the concept of learning from failure. Therefore, following this paradigm, relapsing forward would mean to learn from our relapse experience. Most success management experts often discuss the idea of using pictures or visual props as tools to fuel your vision, dream, change, or goal. The process is simple. Identify where you are trying to go or what you are attempting to achieve. Then find pictures of it or someone who has accomplished it and flood your mind with those images. There are several approaches to this concept. For example, if you decide on a dream home. Take some time on your off day to drive through your ideal residential neighborhood. Scout out the type of home that you desire. I have done this several times. It has always worked for me.

Once you find it, take a picture, or mediate on it in order to get a clear mental vision. Keep that image in your mind as motivation to achieve your goal. This applies to anything. If you are overweight and need to change eating and exercise habits, find a picture of someone who is the size you desire and plaster it on the wall. Go through your closet and find a dress or suit that is too small and make it your goal to get back into that gorgeous dress that once graced your petite figure. The key is to keep reaching forward.

The Apostle Paul, one of the later Christian leaders of the New Testament, wrote many letters to his followers. One letter in particular to a group at a place called Philippi, reveals his teaching on how to focus mental energy toward moving forward in relapse. Paul wrote of his spiritual transformation, destiny, and journey in Philippians 3:12-14, *"Not that I have already attained, or am already perfected; but I press on, that I may lay hold of that for which Christ Jesus has also laid hold of me. Brethren, I do not count myself to have apprehended; but one thing I do, forgetting those things which are behind and reaching forward to those things which are ahead. I press toward the goal for the prize of the upward call of God in Christ Jesus."* (NKJV) In the simple act of forgetting we can find the ability to finish. Life comes with stages and seasons of change.

Second nature to forgetting is the idea and practice of reaching, stretching, aggressively thrusting forward toward what you are striving to achieve. Your strategic plan and smart goals should help assert some accountability at your weakest points. You must know that weakness is a natural response to life. Once you begin to experience depleted willpower and spirituality your resistance can become very low and even fail. When failure hits, remember that it is not final. You can manage that loss with an aggressive rebound and never miss the goal ahead. Failure signals that you are human, not that you are incapable. Your support in succeeding, achieving your goals, managing change, and fulfilling destiny is in your ability to maintain the momentum of your activity until the goal is achieved. In other words, try not to get comfortable. Second, do not back down from your commitment. Third, do not ever quit. All you need are great maintenance skills.

Endgame Maintenance

Let's be honest. When you hear the word relapse, you probably think of someone who has previously abused drugs or alcohol, etc. However, it is worth repeating that relapse is a common failure for people of all walks of life and plagues a broad range of situations and conditions. Relapse simply happens in anyone's attempt to achieve change, success, destiny, goals, or dreams. Relapse is not the ugly, weird, and unwanted topic only discussed in an AA meeting or with a therapist. Relapse is happening every day in the behaviors of people around you. Relapse is common. Avoiding relapse is not. This is why only a small percentage of all New Year's Resolutions is achieved. People are relapsing all the time. Avoidance then requires maintaining your endgame.

In all of my research regarding endgames, I found that it basically means the ending phase of a process or circumstance. In the gaming industry, it is a winning strategy. From the sporting game of chess to the filled football arenas, endgame can be the defining strategic plan or actions to subdue the opponent and gain the victory. Although endgame is an end of the game strategy, it is planned before the game begins or somewhere during the process. The endgame strategy or approach can be applied to achieving your dream, destiny, goal, change or success. It simply requires focusing on the end of a situation before its beginning. Stephen Covey mentions this concept in his book Seven Habits of Highly Effective People. He teaches that effective people begin with the end in mind. Thus, they have an endgame.

Winston Churchill said, *"However beautiful the strategy, you should occasionally look at the results."* What is your endgame? Have you seen the strategy all the way through? One of my sons has played football for most of his life. As a Wide Receiver, his coaches repeatedly taught him over the years the most practical and effective approach to catching a football. It is a simple yet career molding practice. Every coach has told him that when the ball is being thrown to him and he is preparing to catch it to "look the ball all the way in."

This means to focus on the ball, stay focused on the ball, and watch the ball come all the way into your hands completely before you make any attempt to run, juke, or make the next move. It is an endgame to catching the football. See the ball all the way into the end. Your destiny, change, success, dream, goal, or whatever you are striving for is the football that life has given you as an opportunity to receive.

As a Receiver, your number one goal to catching this pass and getting the yardage you need is to have a solid endgame style. You must see this 'ball of opportunity' all the way into your hands until the end. Remember, the endgame must be flexible. You may have to change it in the last few minutes of the fourth quarter or even in overtime. Like the butterfly, the key is structure. Everyone needs the right structure in place to maximize their goals and achieve the endgame.

Chapter Conclusions

1. The Relapse Principle suggests that the potential to return to former stages of behavior is a real threat.

2. The reality of relapse should be understood. Relapse can happen in the "action-stage." Remember, the action stage is when we are most vulnerable. It is when we are closest to change and breakthrough.

3. It is impossible for some physical relapse to happen. *What is possible however is mental and behavioral relapse.* In other words, we can relapse back to some form of habit or way of thinking that we once possessed.

4. *Relapse begins in your mind or within your thoughts.* The simple act of thinking, pondering, and meditating on the wrong action or behavior too long will birth and constitute fulfillment of the thought. Someone once said, *"All action is first conceived in the mind."* Once we believe it, we act on it almost subconsciously.

5. Life comes with stages and seasons of change. Second nature to forgetting is the idea and practice of reaching, stretching, aggressively thrusting forward toward what you are striving to achieve. Your strategic plan and smart goals should help assert some accountability at your weakest points.

6. The endgame strategy or approach can be applied to achieving your dream, destiny, goal, change or success. It simply requires focusing on the end of a situation before its beginning. Stephen Covey mentions this concept in his book Seven Habits of Highly Effective People. He teaches that effective people begin with the end in mind. Thus, they have an endgame.

7. Winston Churchill said, *"However beautiful the strategy, you should occasionally look at the results."* What is your endgame? Have you seen the strategy all the way through? You must see this 'ball of opportunity' all the way into your hands until the end. Can you do it? Do you possess grit? Remember, the endgame must be flexible. You may have to change it in the last few minutes of the fourth quarter or even in overtime.

With good coaching, proper motivation, and the right club structure with organic growth, you can achieve an awful lot in football.

　　　　-Gary Neville, Renowned English Football Player, and Coach

I never went to college. But the structure I grew up with was planted so deep that when it came to doing business, I knew how to be disciplined, create teamwork, and persevere. It set me up to be an entrepreneur and a successful franchiser.

　　　　-Anne F. Beiler, Entrepreneur and Founder of Aunt Annie's

The Principle of Structure suggests that, like wisdom, structure is a universal asset for successful change.

Transformation is a great achievement. Without structure it is prohibited and will ultimately wither and die. Wherever there is change, there is new life. When new life is born, it must be placed within the proper structure in order for it to survive and thrive. Consider the life of a newborn. When a newborn enters the world, this precious new life has to be protected and nurtured by the proper environment and structure. Otherwise, the newborn cannot survive. The newborn is no longer totally feeding off of the nourishment of its old environment. It is no longer comforted with the internal security of the mother's womb. The external forces have the potential to destroy the newborn. The new life in our case is the new person or new accomplishment. Once we aspire to change or mature, we must then identify the proper structure for the new life, person, or accomplishment. Each level of change requires a corresponding structure in order for you to thrive in destiny.

Identify the structure that you need to thrive as the new you. Does the new you or the change require a new level of discipline? Does it require new habits, friends, or level of attention? If you were promoted to management from the labor force, the new you could not survive being co-dependent on the former structure. For example, in this case the labor worker must learn self-management skills as he/she goes from an hourly employee to an exempt employee. Some changes require learning to work independently. Others require learning to work as a team player at the leadership level. In either case, one must learn new people skills and focus on human equity in the organization. When your life change is transitioning from being a "renter" to a "homeowner," you must identify the structure that you need to thrive. A renter typically never has to deal with a homeowner's association. When your life change is transitioning you from single to married, you have to identify the structure necessary to thrive as a husband or wife. You need to learn what it takes to be a good spouse? What structure is necessary to make a house a home? What structure is necessary for healthy communication? Think of it this way, structure equates to life and hope for the future.

Structure Future Dynamics

Tadao Ando, Renown Japanese Architect said, *"If I can create some space that people haven't experienced before and if it stays with them or gives them a dream for the future, that's the kind of structure I seek to create."* Tadao Ando sought to create structures that would impact the imagination and breed hope of possibility. He did it through structures-architectural structures. His goal was not really the building. His goal was the future. By planting seeds of hope and greatness in the minds of those who entered his buildings, he was creating hope and security for a bright future of ideas.

I call this concept the structure future dynamic. You too must design a 'structure'- a life structure that will create hope and security of a bright future. Changing, succeeding, growing, etc. amidst the right structures will amplify your energy and enthusiasm for what can be and what will be for you. It broadens your vision of what is possible. You need this energy and creative thinking in order to stay inspired about what is about to happen in your life.

What is meant by structure is the enabling and support mechanisms that make your change, success, and growth possible. It also means implementing the guidelines and borders that frame your mental pathways and physical energies. It requires creating routines and patterns that carefully function as the escalator to your next level of change, growth, and success. Ask the tough questions. For example, what does the evidence, research, and experts reveal about your strategy, endgame, or journey towards goal achievement? Tough questions will help quantify your growth projections and stabilize your actions, consequently keeping you from failure. When you can see that success is up the road and victory is imminent, it takes the pressure off of getting there and reassures the focus to get it done. Structure is not for the faint of heart.

Protect Your Structure

Children despise structure. Their minds cannot conceive the good at the core of the rules and regulations around them. I understand. They are curious but all curiosity does not need to be explored, just acknowledged. Structure is not about keeping you out; it is about keeping certain things out of you. It is about keeping certain circumstances out of your life, destiny, future, growth, change, and success. I am quite sure you can think of a time when curiosity took you on an unexpected voyage. I can. This has been the prognosis of my foolishness on plenty of occasions. Remember, we are human and not perfect. If you have not failed, fumbled an opportunity, or goofed up a couple of times then you are a human anomaly. You get what I am saying. We all may have goofed up more times than we have gotten it right. Life tends to show us how poor of a grip we have on it. Nevertheless, structure helps you to "put away childish things."

The Apostle Paul, whom I reference quite frequently due in part to his traumatic life and sense of relatability to the common person, instructed his following audience to do the same. To the Church at Corinth he wrote these words, *"When I was a child, I talked like a child, I thought like a child, I reasoned like a child; when I became a man, I did away with childish things."* (1 Corinthians 13:11, AMP) Despite our best efforts, we can all be childish at times. More than we ever really will admit. As you change, as you work on your inner being, and as you focus on getting better in your ambitions, desires, appetites, motives, etc., your soul will prosper and mature for greatness and destiny.

Your mind, will, and emotions will grow in the right direction by leaps and bounds. You will be amazed at the outcome of your maturity level, success, growth, and change. It is essential that the child in us does not die, only in our childish ways.

The child in us is necessary to enjoy life. The childish ways lead to foolish thinking, wasted dreams, and immature behavior.

It is essential to address immaturity, insensitivity, and irresponsibility. They are like cancers that eat away at our transformation. Many people wait for their circumstances or others to change before they grow up or change. Nope. Wrong answer. You are responsible for your life, success, growth or change as well as the lack thereof. You cannot blame- shift here. There is no finger-pointing here. There is no validity in saying, "If this or that would or would not have happened, I could have or would have a, b, and c." This is simply a method of excusing ourselves from responsibility, practicing unforgiveness, and concentrated growth. Structure is a dig-deep concept. It has to come from core values and healthy internal story. The deeper we dig for maturity, the higher our stalk of greatness can grow.

Plant Deep

Since you need structure to survive, thrive, and arrive at success, destiny, goals, change, growth, and greatness, go ahead and plant deep. The latter part of this statement is from Anne F. Beiler's quote in which she gained from her structured childhood. Her childhood structure provided her with discipline, teamwork, and perseverance in place of her lack of education. Although she did not get the formal education that one would assume was needed to achieve her level of success, Anne possessed something that paid off well. Annie was exposed to the right structure. From her own words, discipline, teamwork, and perseverance was the structure, at least part of it. The key to the impact of the structure was that it was planted deeply in her family culture. Structure is useless unless it has measurable impact. You need a structure that will have a lasting and profound impact on you. Not an easy, wimpy, anyone can achieve it structure. Greatness requires a life-changing, gripping, breath-taking, molding structure. A structure like this will automatically stick with you. In other words, it will plant deep. Impactful, molding, gripping, life-changing, deeply planted structure is always preparation for destiny. Are you ready? I hope that you are. If you have gotten this far reading Grow Into Your Greatness, you are about to unearth your next transformation for destiny! Destiny is our next principle.

Chapter Conclusions

1. The Structure Principle suggests that, like wisdom, structure is a universal asset for successful change.

2. Transformation is a great achievement; yet without structure, change is prohibited and will ultimately wither and die. Wherever there is change, there is new life. When new life is born, it must be placed within the proper structure in order for it to survive and thrive.

3. *Identify the structure that you need to thrive as the new you.* Does the new you require a new level of discipline? Does it require new habits, new friends, or level of attention?

4. You too must design a 'structure'- a life structure that will create hope and security of a bright future. Changing, succeeding, growing, etc. amidst the right structures will amplify your energy and enthusiasm for what can be possible.

5. Structure is not about keeping you out; it is about keeping certain things out of you. It is about keeping certain circumstances out of your life, destiny, future, growth, change, and success.

6. The Apostle Paul, whom I reference quite frequently due in part to his traumatic life and sense of relatability to the common person, instructed his following audience to do the same. To the Church at Corinth he wrote these words, "When I was a child, I talked like a child, I thought like a child, I reasoned like a child; when I became a man, I did away with childish things." (1 Corinthians 13:11, AMP)

7. Structure is not beneficial unless it has impact. You need a structure that will have a lasting and profound impact on you. Not an easy, wimpy, anyone can achieve it structure. But a life changing, gripping, breathtaking, molding structure. A structure like this will automatically stick with you. In other words, it will plant deeply. List what you need in your structure and go after it.

As long as we are persistent in our pursuit of our deepest destiny, we will continue to grow. We cannot choose the day or time when we will fully bloom. It happens in its own time.

-Denis Waitley, Author, and Motivational Speaker

It is in your moments of decision that your destiny is shaped.

-Tony Robbins, Success Mentor and Author

Chapter 19

The Destiny Principle

The Destiny Principle suggests that you are internally assigned and appointed to flourish in a particular place, at an appointed time, and to a specified cause.

Before furthering our discussion about the destiny principle, what exactly is destiny to you? I particularly understand destiny means living a life that is in alignment or agreement with your God-breathed purpose, intimate passions, core values, gifts, and talents. Destiny can be illusive without the right internal guidance system. Without the proper internal guidance system, you can arrive at the wrong location. And even do so for the rest of your life. People end up here all the time. Why do you think so many people retire with regret? In a recent study of a large group of elderly people who were approaching the end of their lives, they were given a survey asking what they regretted most at the end of their lives. The unanimous answer was not what they had done but what they had not done.

Brian Tracy, in his book Change Your Thinking Change Your Life wrote, *"If you would quit your current job if you won a million dollars this is a danger signal. It means that you are in great danger of wasting your career and wasting your life."* This rings true of other areas in your life. Destiny can be illusive. Even with the right internal guidance system, discovering destiny can take some time. We often have to weed out hyper self-ambition, greed, opinion, and plain old confusion due to traumatic experience.

In his book, Destiny, the creative and profound author T.D. Jakes wrote, *"God has already implanted in you the raw materials needed to shape destiny into reality. You already have what's needed to actualize your vision for life. It is a God-given vision; otherwise, you would not have it."* For this reason, it is a necessity to choose God as the voice of your internal guidance system. He is the Creator and Sustainer of Life. Our environment and the outcome of our destiny can be determined by a lot of factors; however, I am convinced that it is God who fulfills the destination. Before an egg becomes an adult butterfly, the one who cares the most, the adult butterfly, assigns it an environment. The one who cares the most about you, God, The Father, has assigned you an environment called destiny. The environment is specifically designed to foster the growth and success of the egg. If not, it would be an unfruitful and unsuccessful match. Destiny is a fit. You will know destiny when it is a sure fit for you.

God's Plan Is Best

God has the best plan of destiny for us. He has the perfect fit. In speaking through one of the major Old Testament Prophets named Jeremiah, He said, *"For I know the plans and thoughts that I have for you, plans for peace and well-being and not for disaster to give you a future and a hope."* (Jeremiah 29:11, Amplified Bible) Is that amazing, overwhelming, and great news? God does not have a plan of disaster for us but a future (destiny) of peace and well-being. Jeremiah 29:11 encompasses many of the subjects that we have mentioned in previous chapters. In previous chapters we discussed principles which included having a plan, establishing well-being, avoiding the threat of annihilation, envisioning an ideal future, and the value of hope. Although we've discussed spirituality moderately, we need the Holy Spirit to lead and guide us into the plan and will of God. First, it requires making Jesus your Lord and Savior. This is the first step in creating intimacy with the Holy Spirit as our Guide. Jesus said of the Holy Spirit in John 14:26, *"But the Helper (Comforter, Advocate, Intercessor— Counselor, Strengthener, Standby), the Holy Spirit, whom the Father will send in My name [in My place, to represent Me and act on My behalf], He will teach you all things. And He will help you remember everything that I have told you."* (AMP) I am asking you to forget all of the naysayers and focus on faith in God. When you entrust your heart and hope to God, He will always steer you in the right direction. The wisdom in His direction leads to every destination we are assigned and appointed.

Many people get overly anxious about destiny. They even grow fearful and worry themselves sick about missing destiny. Others become compulsive and obsessed about destiny. It becomes the focal point of much of their spiritual conversation. I know because I was the latter. I know because I've led and pastored Christians for decades. You do not have to chase destiny. Chase God! Destiny will reveal itself when we have transformed from the inside out. One Chinese proverb says, "When the student is ready, the teacher will appear." (Author Unknown) Are you ready? Are you willing to start the internal contemplation and to move into action? Trust God! He will always guide you into who you are destined to be. He has the best plan.

What are some practical steps that you can employ to aid in identifying and uncovering the destiny that God has breathed into your existence? Tony Robbins, Success Mentor and Author, suggests that your decisions determine your destiny. Darren Hardy wrote in his book, The Compound Effect, *"Your life is the product of your moment-to-moment choices."* We need the Holy Spirit's wisdom to guide our everyday decisions from moment-to-moment. Destiny is not as simple as making day to day decisions based on the merit of our wisdom apart from God. There has to be more. I am convinced that God is in no way short of ways to get us to our destiny. The process, however, always begins within. Brian Tracy offers this solution as a practical approach to identifying who you are. Here are some questions to consider from his book, Change Your Thinking Change Your Life.

- What are your core competencies?
- What special talents and abilities set you apart from others?
- What would I choose to work at if I were financially independent and could do anything I wanted?
- What do you love doing?
- Looking back on your past, what sorts of activities have given you the greatest results and rewards?
- Define what gives you the feeling of most importance.

Answering these questions honestly and thoughtfully will help but it is the Internal Guidance System of the Holy Spirit that will order your steps. Proverbs 20:24 says, *"Man's steps are ordered and ordained by the Lord. How then can a man [fully] understand his way?"* (AMP) I recall studying about purpose and destiny for a lecture. I ran across a saying that goes like this,

"Anyone with anger and passion about a problem and wants to see it fixed has found a clue to destiny and purpose." Without the Holy Spirit we are left with clues without closure. Choose closure!

Surviving Surroundings

Adult butterflies thrive in a specific, nourishing environment. Oftentimes, the same elements present through the egg stage of change are also present in the adult stage of the caterpillar change. The egg is nourished from the base nutrients of the environment, but the adult butterfly thrives off of the superior elements of the environment. The adult butterfly does not need what the egg needs, but the elements for both can exist within the same environment. This is why one can start out employed as a mail clerk in a business yet retire as the CEO of the same company years later. The same environment that nurtured the mail clerk has also nurtured the CEO. How the mail clerk got to this destination in the first place is a matter of internal assignment and appointment to flourish in a particular place and to a specified cause.

It is foolish to think that an environment has to change in order for one to survive and thrive successfully once they have transformed. Environments create new skills, attitudes, and abilities. I am convinced that God is the author of placing everyone and everything in the proper environment. After all, He is the author of destiny. Who can account for the flowers in the field or the stars in the sky? Who can measure the depths of the sea or the caverns of the earth? Who has numbered the animals of the earth or discovered the vastness of the galaxies abroad? What man has tackled the deepest ability of the human brain or even formed an original thought? It is God alone who ordains man's steps and calls him into wonderful places to grow, shine, and prosper.

He raises kings up and sets them low. He gives us gifts, talents, and skills that make room for us and bring us before great men. It is our free will and decisions that can place us in the wrong or threatening environment. Our only responsibility relative to environment is learning to identify when we are in the wrong one, for the right one will be revealed by God. How do we determine when we are in the wrong or unnourishing environment? Here is what to look for with the wrong environment:

- Does this environment foster growth?
- Does this environment have enough and more than enough to supply for my needs?
- Does this environment reflect who I am or who I am not?
- Does this environment abuse or celebrate my unique being?
- Does this environment hold me back or thrust me forward?
- Does this environment challenge as well as comfort me?
- Does this environment produce others like me?
- Does this environment protect or threaten?
- Does the climate of this environment suit my growth ecosystem?

Climate Change

Climate speaks to the personality and culture of the people and conditions of an environment. Nature climate and conditions can be hot, cold, dark, light, wet, dry, etc. Figuratively speaking, is the climate of your environment too dark? Meaning is it evil, lack moral substance, or fair opportunity for you to thrive? Is your climate figuratively too cold? Does it lack the warmth of love, altruism, or acceptance? Is it transformational or transactional? Do people act robotically? We have to determine a reasonable solution for climate control. Gauging how to examine or produce a healthy climate requires truth, courage, and action. Climate is essential. When the climate is too cold the butterfly dies. If the conditions are too dry the fish lifespan diminishes. The butterfly's climate has to support its' reproductivity.

You will know each time that you are at the right destination because of the quality and quantity of your reproduction. When opportunity meets destiny, reproduction occurs. It is a flammable combustion engineered by the relationship between what is in you and the need of your environment. Check for reproduction quality. When that combustible energy does not exist, then you may not be evolving, changing, growing, or fulfilling destiny and purpose. Dependence upon your internal guidance system, which is none more accurate than the Holy Spirit, can make the difference between waisted time and vested time. Climates can change. As a matter of fact, one can experience several climates and conditions in the same day.

Dr. Jerrell Stokley Jr.

The Holy Spirit is valuable in helping us determine if we are dealing with a temporary or permanent climate. In addition, He can empower us to positively shift, change, or impact and unproductive climate. The climate may be your assignment. We can't be too quick to write off a climate without first confirming if it is ours to reengineer.

Chapter Conclusions

1. The Destiny Principle suggests that you are internally assigned and appointed to flourish in a particular place, at an appointed time, and to a specified cause.

2. I particularly understand destiny means living a life that is in alignment or agreement with your God-breathed purpose, intimate passions, core values, gifts, and talents. Destiny can be illusive without the right internal guidance system.

3. In his book, Destiny, the creative and profound author T.D. Jakes wrote, *"God has already implanted in you the raw materials needed to shape destiny into reality. You already have what's needed to actualize your vision for life. It is a God-given vision; otherwise, you would not have it."*

4. God has the best plan of destiny for us. He has the perfect fit. In speaking through one of the major Old Testament Prophets named Jeremiah, He said, "For I know the plans and thoughts that I have for you, plans for peace and well-being and not for disaster to give you a future and a hope." (Jeremiah 29:11, Amplified Bible)

5. Tony Robbins, Success Mentor and Author, suggests that your decisions determine your destiny. Darren Hardy wrote in his book, The Compound Effect, "Your life is the product of your moment-to-moment choices." We need the Holy Spirit's wisdom to guide our everyday decisions from moment-to-moment.

6. The adult butterfly does not need what the egg needs but the elements for both can exist within the same environment. This is why one can start out employed as a mail clerk in a business yet retire as the CEO of the same company years later. The same environment that nurtured the mail clerk has also nurtured the CEO.

7. You will know each time that you are at the right destination because of the quality and quantity of your reproduction. When opportunity meets destiny, reproduction occurs. It is a flammable combustion engineered by the relationship between what is in you and the need of your environment. Check for reproduction quality.

Circumstances are beyond human control, but our conduct is in our own power.

-Benjamin Disraeli, Writer, and British Prime Minister

Laws control the lesser man... Right conduct controls the greater one.

-Mark Twain, Author, and Inventor

Chapter 20

The Behavior Principle

The Behavior Principle suggests the same species will ultimately live out the same behavior.

In his book The Compound Effect, Darren Hardy wrote, "*What stands between you and your goals is your behavior…That's why it's imperative to figure out which behaviors are blocking the path that leads to your goal, and which behavior will help you accomplish your goal.*" Human nature is drawn to congregate, migrate, and fraternize with others. We are societal people. We were created to be interdependent upon each other and the system we create. Thus, the old adage, "No man is an island." It's a catchy way of saying that we need one another. Behavior is a product of learning patterns, beliefs, and coping skills. We repeat as adults whatever we learned during our formative years as children. Our childhood behaviors, passed down from relatives, become a type of hardwired system controlling our responses, perceptions, and interpretations. So, our thought life is conditioned to reflect the teachings of whomever molded us. We became a mirror image of them. We ultimately develop our unique personality and difference, yet in many ways still reflect their behavior.

We can carry childhood trauma and dysfunction into our adulthood because we have subconsciously mastered behaviors that reflect that trauma or dysfunction. This is also true of positive child rearing and a supportive family environment. It goes without saying that we become the company that we keep. In order to develop behavior patterns that lead to greatness, destiny, purpose, and growth, we must surround ourselves with teachers who emulate the character traits that we need. When you want to be successful, find out who is successful in the area that you desire, then do

183

what successful people do. You will ultimately migrate to and around those in which you feel most comfortable.

The challenge is to understand and be mindful of the reality that we become a combination of our reference group. You want to find the right reference group for our growth, change, success, destiny, and purpose. This may require a courageous act of change. Although there are inferior and superior types in any species, the majority of the species behave the same. The behavior of the butterfly is conducive to others of its species. Though uniquely designed and different from any other, its distinctive behavior aligns with that of others cut from the same cloth and born from the same DNA. I'm sure you know that DNA is a chemical chain that transfers characteristics throughout generations. I heard it once said that "Birds of a feather flock together." Others have said, "You are the sum total of the circle of people you keep." In social cultures I have heard it said that "the apple does not fall too far from the tree." These sayings did not pop up out of nowhere. They are backed by scientific and social truths.

Reference Groups

Brian Tracy, author of the book, Change Your Thinking Change Your Life, teaches about reference groups quite often. Brian says of reference groups, *"Your reference group is defined as the people you consider yourself to be similar to."* The Behavior Principle is associated with identity. Believe it or not, we are the sum total of those people that we designate as most important to us and with whom we spend most of our time. Your reference group helps shape your identity or lack thereof. When we know who we are, we know how and what behavior to apply. Yet, when we are lost in our identity, we conform to the base thoughts and behaviors within and without. Thus, it is important to learn the behaviors that compliment your success. They will be the DNA for habits at your next level of transformation and destiny. Tracy writes of reference groups that, *"Over time, through a process of absorption, you will adopt their attitudes, mannerisms, ways of speaking, levels of aspiration, and even their style of dress. Your reference group will exert an inordinate influence on the kind of person you become."*

What are the behaviors necessary to succeed at your current and next stage of transformation? What books do you need to read? What seminars do you need to attend? What challenges do you need to take on? What additional changes do you need to make? What are your continual growth areas? How do people at the stage of change and success in which you aspire steward influence, wealth, time, and vision? How do they produce without excuse? Monitoring your behavior is critical to staying in alignment with the core values that create stability and healthy growth. What does it take for you to identify and maintain the right core values?

I use the word species very lightly. Species in this sense refers to the type of person you are or seeking to become. For example, I will use Christians as a "species." What are the behaviors and core values for an individual to thrive as a Christian? Faith? Love? Compassion? There is an understood and proven, truthful foundation for Christian core values and behavior. The same applies to other species. For example, what are the behaviors and core values of a successful small business entrepreneur, educator, author, engineer, or church planter? Let's entertain each one as species. When you identify the cloth that you are cut from, then you can begin to identify the DNA of the species.

When we learn their patterns, beliefs, and coping skills, we organically reproduce their behavior. When referencing transformation of our character, Dallas Willard and Don Simpson, Authors of the book Revolution of Character, wrote, *"My character is me. Character is that internal, overall structure of our self that reveals our long-running patterns of behavior...Our character can change."* Since "character is me," who are you? Your behavior says it all.

Success Patterns

Since we live in the world with others, behavior is important to success. Therefore, one must quickly assimilate toward proven patterns of successful behavior.

The Golden Rule is one behavior we should seek to master. Harry J. Gensler, in his book Ethics, wrote, *"To apply the Golden Rule, you'd imagine yourself in another person's place on the receiving end of the action."* The key is what you practice in private you produce in public. Create uniformity and balance between your private and public practice and you will consistently produce successful behavior. When you know who you are, you know what behavior to apply. Behavior communicates our emotional intelligence. Emotional intelligence is the science and art of self-awareness, self-management, and social responsibility. We can only manage the behavior of which we are keenly aware. Self-awareness is how in tune we are with our emotions, responses, and relationship skills.

Self-management is how well we control and change our emotions to achieve healthy relationships. In other words, emotional intelligence can determine and predict how well we fair with our social environment. Can you now see why behavior is the backdrop of success? Henry David Thoreau, Author, and Philosopher, once said, *"I know of no more encouraging fact than the unquestionable ability of man to elevate his life by conscious endeavor."* In reality, you alone are responsible for your behavior and decisions. Your efforts or lack thereof to achieve a high level of emotional intelligence should not be overlooked by blaming, inward consideration, identification, or justification. The most successful approach is one that starts with you and ends with you. Stephen Covey, Author of the book Seven Habits of Highly Effective People, defines responsibility as the ability to choose your response. Hence the word response-ability. Mastering behavior boils down to responsibility and a good conscience. As a child growing up, I would frequently indulge in a little eavesdropping of adult conversations, as most children do.

Periodically, I would hear an adult say, "My conscience is clear because I did it with a good conscience." Have you ever heard anyone say this? Have you ever said it yourself? If so, you were communicating that your actions were responsible and well-intended. Consequently, the key to successful behavior. Covey explains that *"We have a conscience – a deep inner awareness of right and wrong, of the principles that govern our behavior, and a sense of the degree to which our thoughts and actions are in harmony with them."* How about you? Are you keenly aware of your behavior? Are there behaviors that are ruining your relationships? How successful are you at being self-aware and managing that self-awareness? Practicing the disciplines, actions, decisions, and mindsets of those who have achieved their intended destiny and level of success is critical. Go after those behaviors.

Rabbi Daniel Lapin, Radio Talk-Show Host and Author, wrote in his book Thou Shalt Prosper, *"Convert change from enemy to ally by understanding when to enjoy the exhilaration of change and when to fight it and steadfastly defend the unchangeable."*

Of course, all change is not good. Thus, the reason why other-initiated or self-initiated change can be painful depending on its impact and outcome. Nevertheless, you have the sole responsibility of determining how you respond to the painful other-initiated or self-initiated change. You are aware that some changes you have made caused some of life's pains, aren't you? I hope that you are or else you have blamed everyone and everything else for all that has happened in your life. And that is just not true. Finding balance with change will give you contentment with change. Some change may affect you but need not be welcomed by you. You have to know the difference.

Chapter Conclusions

1. The Behavior Principle suggests the same species will ultimately live out the same behavior.

2. *"What stands between you and your goals is your behavior…That's why it's imperative to figure out which behaviors are blocking the path that leads to your goal, and which behavior will help you accomplish your goal."* (Darren Hardy, The Compound Effect)

3. Brian Tracy, author of the book, Change Your Thinking Change Your Life, teaches about reference groups quite often. Brian says of reference groups, *"Your reference group is defined as the people you consider yourself to be similar to."*

4. In addition, Brian writes, *"Over time, through a process of absorption, you will adopt their attitudes, mannerisms, ways of speaking, levels of aspiration, and even their style of dress. Your reference group will exert an inordinate influence on the kind of person you become."* (MJF Books, 2003)

5. What are the behaviors necessary to succeed at your current and next stage of change? What books do you need to read? What seminars do you need to attend? What challenges do you need to take on? What additional changes do you need to make? What are your continual growth areas? How do people at the stage of change and success in which you aspire steward influence, wealth, time, and vision? How do they produce without excuse?

6. Create uniformity and balance between your private and public practice and you will discover consistent behavior. When you know who you are, you know what behavior to apply. Your behavior communicates how emotionally intelligent you are. Emotional intelligence is the science and art of self-awareness, self-management, and social responsibility.

7. You are aware that some changes you have made caused some of life's pains, aren't you? I hope that you are or else you have blamed everyone and everything else for all that has happened in your life. And that is

just not true. Finding balance with change will give you contentment with change. Some change may affect you but need not be welcomed by you. You have to know the difference.

It is not possible to win high-level success without meeting opposition, hardship, and setback. But it is possible to use setbacks to propel you forward.
                                                              -David J. Schwartz, Author

Sometimes when you innovate, you make mistakes. It is best to admit them quickly and get on with improving your other innovations.
                                              -Steve Jobs, Entrepreneur, and Inventor

Chapter 21

The Renewal Principle

The Renewal Principle suggests that survival and long-term stability requires new identity and habits.

In his book, Reposition Yourself, Bishop T. D. Jakes, gives insightful perspective regarding how change and renewal interrelate. He says, *"It's prudent, practical, and the golden key to throwing off the limits of your past failures and repositioning yourself into the sweet spot of success."* What do you do when you have peaked out in an area of change and your only way to thrive is renewal? Oftentimes when we reach this point, we have matured in such finality in one area or another that our only resolve is to start over, lay a new foundation, launch a new department or product line, reinvent self, enlarge social circles, etc. I like to call this the Breaking Point. Life tends to challenge everyone with breaking points. Breaking points challenge our ability to lay everything on the line and face our greatest challenges. Breaking points are times and seasons when we simply have no choice but to start over. Who enjoys starting over? Who enjoys learning new skills, processes, and expertise when past practices have provided comfort and profit? Who likes being a "newbie" all over again?

The average person regrets, despises, and even avoids progressing if it means starting over. Starting over can feel like misery if you succumb to your emotions. Nevertheless, when you really analyze the cost of failure, you quickly align yourself with the necessary changes of survival. For example, as technology evolved in the United States, the music industry faced drastic changes putting some companies completely out of business. To this end, individuals were stuck with the choice to either throw in the towel and quit or reinvent the company to keep up with the changing technological world in order to make a profit. The Principle of Renewal demands attention on every level of life. A single mom who suddenly is faced with a handicap child has to address starting over in an at-home career or readjusting life to fit the new situation. The college student, after high school graduation, has to renew a sense of independence as he or she moves away from home and starts a new journey. An aging businessperson has to learn new skills in the health care industry to compete with the younger health care experts graduating from Ivy League universities. Regardless of who you are or what your life status, renewal will always play a key role in how long you last or what type of legacy you leave behind. The key to successful renewal is developing resistance to the pain of renewal and the courage to engage in the process.

Seasons Change

Each season flowers grow and bloom and express their beauty. Their beauty appeals to our senses, and we are mesmerized. Because of our gratitude for the flowers' beauty, it almost seems sad when the season changes. Day by day, we slowly watch the pedals repeatedly fall to the ground until there is nothing left but the stem from which the beautiful flower once flourished. However, do not feel sorrow for the flower. Its beauty shall return. In order for renewal to happen some things must fall off so that new things can replace them. When we can shift our focus from what we have lost to what is sprouting up in the new season, we live in the enchantment of purpose and destiny. Do not feel sorry for yourself when you have to start over and renew. Your beauty shall return. Your dreams shall live again. Your wealth will return. Your hope will flourish. Your season will come to pass.

Birds are interesting species to watch. I often gaze out of the windows of my home watching birds interact. Birds are resilient and resourceful. They can get great use and support from the smallest, overlooked objects-like grass or mud. Birds can teach us a valuable lesson about the courage to start over, develop resistance, and endure painful processes. There was once a bird's nest above a column on my back porch. It was built in a cool, secluded area with much shade and protection from other birds and predators. The nest belonged to what appeared to be a bird family. It was obviously built rather quickly or at least without much of my attention because I do not recall seeing the process although the window in which I gazed was my favorite. I love looking at the beauty of nature-its trees, flowers, grass, and the beauty of the sky. Although I watch nature and birds, etc., I am not a fan of coming in contact with birds or wildlife. Once we discovered the bird's' nest, we deemed it an intrusion. Whenever anyone opened our back door to partake of the serene backyard atmosphere or the inviting outdoor furniture, the birds would release this screeching sound, flap their wings and flutter away to a nearby location while keeping a close eye on the nest. Obviously, it was their home. Yet their home became an invasion of ours.

Desiring to protect the birds and enjoy our area too, we decided to ask a friend to come by and find a new home for the bird family. Soon, he stopped by and removed the nest to a nearby spot. The nest was gone, and we had our serene atmosphere back. It at least appeared that way. A day or so afterwards, while looking out of the window gazing at the beauty of nature, I noticed a nest in the exact location of the one we had removed. In that nest was the same bird family. Well, you can imagine what I decided to do. Yes, you are correct. I called that same friend, and he kindly removed the nest for the second time. The battle between the birds and me for the perfect home was over. I won. Well, not exactly! A day or two later the bird rebuilt the nest for the third time. By this time, I was getting the message. The bird understood the principle of renewal. The bird family had developed a resistance to the pain of starting over and willingly employed the courage to do so. In the end, I won but the principle was well understood.

The birds cannot nest there anymore. Phillip is sitting there now. Who is Phillip? Phillip is a brand of paint. I used an empty paint can in order to block space along ledge where the nest was repeatedly built. It is now positioned on the ledge to prevent the next bird renovation. Like the bird, you will win some and you will lose some. Either way, the value is in learning life lessons along the journey. You may find an obstacle that prevents your renovation. The good news is that the bird simply relocated and renewed the renovation somewhere else. When one door shuts, another opens. Especially, when you look for it.

Practicing a few keys disciplines can be greatly resourceful in renewal process.

- Combat fear with courage and productivity. Don't overthink the process and move forward to the new thing.
- Practice enthusiasm. Do not lull yourself into procrastination and apathy. Self-pity will get you nowhere fast.
- Focus on solutions. No need to focus on problems. When you do, it distracts your attention from the future.
- Do not blame and point fingers. Take responsibility. It is the greatest discipline to success.
- Be persistent. Starting over is not easy, but it is possible. It will get tough at times, but persistence will bring you through.
- Manage emotions with intelligence. A clear, well-thought-out plan is the only way to survival. It will keep your hope and dreams alive.
- Evaluate each stage of progress. This will ensure that your foundation is solid and that your plan is working.

The Principle of Renewal says that you can start over successfully, but you must first learn from your past mistakes rather than sulk at them. Reignite the fire of determination in you. Resolve to be creative and start over with intentionality. There is no one who can stop you when you set your mind to achieve anything. The only barrier to a fresh start and significant renewal is your perspective of your situation. Remember, your thoughts determine what direction you take. Everything about your success, change, purpose, dreams, and goals is tied to the way you think. Think successful and you will be. Think courageously and you will find courage. From what I have learned most successful people have actually failed more times than they have succeeded. Be relentless. Start over. Get back up. Be an architect of change. Finish well. Birth the new you! Rebrand, reinvent, and renew.

Chapter Conclusions

1. The Principle of Renewal suggests that mastering change is not enough; one must also practice a new state of being or habit for survival and long-term profitability.

2. What do you do when you have peaked out in an area of change and your only mode of survival is that you find a way to keep growing? Oftentimes when we reach this point, we have matured in such finality in one area or another that our only resolve is to start over, lay a new foundation, pick up more contracts, reinvent self, become more social, etc. I like to call this The Breaking Point.

3. The average person regrets, despises, and even avoids progressing if it means starting over. Starting over can feel like misery if you succumb to your emotions. Nevertheless, when you really analyze the cost of failure, you quickly align yourself with the necessary changes of survival.

4. In order for renewal to happen some things must fall off in order for new things to replace them. When we can shift our focus from what we have lost or what has fallen off to what is sprouting up in the new season or what is to come in the future, we can once again live in the enchantment of the beauty contained within a life of purpose and destiny.

5. The bird understood the principle of renewal. The bird family had developed a resistance to the pain of starting over and willingly deployed the courage to do so.

6. Do not blame and point fingers. Take responsibility for your life. It is the greatest discipline to success. Be persistent. Starting over is not easy, but it is possible. It will be tough at times, but persistence will bring you through. Manage emotions with intelligence. A clear, well-thought-out plan is the only way to survival. It will keep your hope and dreams alive.

7. Think successful and you will be successful. Think courageously and you will find courage. From what I have learned, most successful people have actually failed more times than they have succeeded. Be relentless. Start over. Get back up. Be an architect of change. Finish well. Birth the new you. Rebrand. Reinvent. Renew.

Every test, every trial, every heartache that's been significant, I can turn it over and see how God has turned it into good no matter what.

-Charles Stanley,

There can only be one state of mind as you approach any profound test: total concentration, a spirit of togetherness, and strength.

-Pat Riley, NBA Basketball Player, and Coach

Chapter 22

The Testing Principle

The Testing Principle suggests that tests will come.

Did you know that every product, service, and theory must be tested for sustainability before released to the general public? It is true. Do you remember how you were tested on every subject and most information that you learned in school? Have you considered the power of testing? Testing reinforces success. Once a product, theory, service, or knowledge has been tested and proven true, success with it is highly probable. As you change and come into "the new you" you will be tested at each new level of change. Any formative test that is designed to reveal weakness and improve strengths can be arduous. Especially, when the reward or outcome is great. In addition, God often allows us to be tested to reveal our heart posture. Tests are mirrors that reflect our core condition. Consider the Jewish people, whom God tested during their delivers from Egyptian slavery. In summary of their test Deuteronomy 8:2 (NIV) says, "Remember how the Lord your God led you all the way in the wilderness these forty years, to humble and test you in order to know what was in your heart, whether or not you would keep his commands." The Jews experienced forty years of testing as God labored with grace and patience to transform them into a great nation. He was after the greatness within them. The true elixir of greatness is testing.

As you experience new seasons, depths, heights, and dimensions, those dimensions come with added responsibilities and maintenance. Some schools of thought contend that the final stage of change in the psychology of behavior is maintaining. Maintaining means keeping a level of success, growth, or consistency. The temptations to fall short of maintaining can become quite challenging. This was also the test for the Jewish people.

They displayed moments of faith in God and Moses' leadership. However, they lacked the consistency to enter into their greatest self. Therefore, they couldn't be matured in the faith and wisdom to access their greatest destiny and harvest. They were consistently tempted with the desire to revert back to slavery and the lifestyle of Egypt. Temptation rarely ceases. It is relentless. The Principle of Relapse suggests that there is always the real threat of falling back into old habits and ways. Life forces, adversaries, toxins, and predators survive off of our demise rather than to starve from our success and growth. There will always be tests that come to try your ability to remain fruitful and bountiful in any area of success or growth.

Change itself is a tester. Life and circumstances change often. When they do, our intelligence, willpower, determination, perspective, optimism, emotional intelligence, knowledge, skills, and more is tested. As a matter of fact, our tests will come from within and without. As human beings we often push ourselves to be better and do better by testing our limits. The greatest tests are often those that are out of your control. It is important to expect difficulty and understand that what is learned must be tested. What is earned must be proved. Normal Vincent Peal once said, *"When God wants to send you a big gift, he wraps it up in a problem. The bigger the gift that God wants to send you, the bigger the problem he wraps it up in."* In some cases, it is important to welcome tests. Maintaining a posture of growth requires the expectancy of test. Good tests are designed to grant us access to power and influence. Psalm 26:2 (NASB) says, *"Examine me, O' Lord, and try me. Test my mind and my heart."* God looks into our heart and examines who we really are and what we really need. For this reason alone, our transformation can be difficult for us to understand. As ill-equipped readers of our own heart, God often takes us down paths of growth that we fail to realize we need. One Chinese Proverb says, *"When the student is ready, the teacher will appear."* Testing serves as a trainer. It can be the sparring partner of life that improves our toughest core abilities and works the muscles of our learning skills. When you learn to succeed at passing tests, you can process through change, growth, destiny, purpose, and success with contentment and focus.

When you fail at passing tests, you can fall into the hellacious abyss of discontentment, complaining, and negativity. Which do you prefer? The better question may be which are you right now? Have you learned that everything will be tested? Your relationships, health, finances, career, belief, knowledge, self-concept, everything! Everything will be tested over and over again. In church, we say, "New levels equal new devils." In other words, there is always a trainer, tempter, or opponent at every stage, age, and dimension of life. Your trainer will appear! Your trainer has been appearing over and over all of your life and will continue to appear whether you agree, like it, or approve. From now on when testing and trouble arise or appear, try to acknowledge it. Say to yourself, "My trainer is here." I know it is easier said than done, but most things are, right? You have succeeded before. You will succeed again.

Accept the words of Jesus Christ. He said in John 16:33 (Amplified Bible), *"In the world you will have tribulation, distress, and suffering, but be courageous (be confident, be undaunted, be filled with joy); I have overcome the world. My conquest is accomplished, my victory abiding."* Let's face it, life is full of tests, but you can overcome them. We can overcome them. Success also brings tests. Franchising a business does not come without tests. Getting engaged does not come without tests. Obtaining a post graduate degree does not come without tests. Our comfort rests in the fact that with every test we evolve into a better person when we pass. We can evolve into a better person when we fail, if we choose to learn from that failure. Tests bring change. Change brings tests. We cannot experience one without the other. A community exploding with growth signifies a community undergoing test. One test is can the residents manage new neighbors and diversity well. Can the street demographics accommodate the increase of traffic? Are schools able to manage a spike in student attendance? All significant change, good or bad, brings tests.

No Pain No Purpose

Weighing the cost of your pain against the reward of purpose or the overarching goal will extend your pain threshold. This formula alone will help you pass where you would otherwise fail. A close look at what you have come out of and how far you have climbed will empower you to finish. Remember, "Quitters never win, and winners never quit." Supply yourself with enough willpower and ferocious attitude to look into the face of adversity and give it a sucker punch. When you refuse to give up, life will regurgitate your blessings, success, opportunity, and greatness. You will have to defeat the odds set against you. I know this process all too well. I have done it time and time again. I should be a statistic. I have been the underdog more times than I can count. I have looked into the face of misery, disappointment, insanity, and discouragement and sucker punched them. It is a necessity that the world gets the opportunity to benefit from your unique design, precious personality, and divine greatness.

Go after your change, purpose, destiny, growth, and success with everything in you and some. Develop the grit and fortitude for what you believe you can have and who you believe that you are destined to become. Why not? You are unstoppable, right? You are relentless, right? I mean really, if we were sitting face to face having this discussion, who in the world could you say can honestly stop you? Right. I agree. No one. Now, go be relentless and greet your trainer with a smile. Develop yourself to be great and you will be great indeed.

Chapter Conclusions

1. The Principle of Testing suggests that tests will come.

2. Some schools of thought contend that the final stage of change in the psychology of behavior is maintaining. Maintaining means keeping a level of success, growth, or consistency. The temptations to fall short of maintaining can become quite challenging.

3. Life and circumstances change often. When they do, your intelligence, willpower, determination, perspective, optimism, emotional intelligence, knowledge, skills, and more will be tested.

4. Normal Vincent Peal once said, *"When God wants to send you a big gift, he wraps it up in a problem. The bigger the gift that God wants to send you, the bigger the problem he wraps it up in."*

5. One Chinese Proverb says, *"When the student is ready, the teacher will appear."* Testing serves as a trainer. It can be the sparring partner of life that improves our toughest core abilities and works the muscles of our learning skills.

6. Weighing the cost of your pain against the reward of purpose or the overarching goal will extend your pain threshold. This formula alone will help you pass where you would otherwise fail.

7. Supply yourself with enough willpower and ferocious attitude to look into the face of adversity and give it a sucker punch. When you refuse to give up, life will regurgitate your blessings, success, opportunity, and greatness. You must defeat the odds set against you.

Top success is reserved for the I-can-do-it-better kind of person.
                    -Dr. David J. Schwartz, Professor and Author

If you wish to achieve worthwhile things in your personal and career life, you must become a worthwhile person in your own self-development.
                    -Brian Tracy, Success Mentor and Author

Chapter 23

The Power of Self-Development

Self-development is the practice of investing in your personal and professional growth through proven strategies and tested wisdom.

The Apostle Peter, a key figure in the Bible, taught his Jewish Christian audience how to apply this principle to avoid getting stagnate in their faith. The principle is universal and can be applied to any area of life. He wrote in 2 Peter 1:5-8 (NASB), "*Now for this very reason also, applying all diligence, in your faith supply moral (g)excellence, and in your moral excellence, knowledge, and in your knowledge, self-control, and in your self-control, perseverance, and in your perseverance, godliness, and in your godliness, brotherly kindness, and in your brotherly kindness, love. For if these qualities are yours and are increasing, they render you neither useless nor unfruitful in the true knowledge of our Lord Jesus Christ.*" We can learn a lot from this passage. It highlights the value of being diligent in self-development. Peter advocates for his readers to be the one responsible for adding to what they already have and doing so with diligence. Without doing so, they risk remaining stagnate and blind to what could be. Who you are and who you could become are trapped or released by your unwillingness or willingness to continually grow.

When I learned this principle, my life, wisdom, reasoning, willpower, belief, progress, determination, focus, and much more improved drastically. I have not found a way to sustain more control over myself or my path to destiny than the principle of self-development. No other principle in the success psychology space has super charged my success and self-awareness path more than this one. This is the crème de la crème of all success principles. It is absolutely powerful. Investing in your growth shifts you out of terminally nesting in the realm of familiarity and comfort into the deepest waters of belief, courage, and faith to succeed. Someone once said, "Anything that is not growing is either fake or dying." Self-development, be it spiritual or otherwise, is the key to transformation, advancement, destiny, purpose, and exponential growth. Self-development has made poor men rich. Self-development has made ignorant men wise. Self-development has birthed innovators of world change and technological advancements. Self-development has produced iconic global leaders and international game-changers. Depending on others to create a system or write a program for your personal development and growth potential is irresponsible and immature. However, building off the foundation of history's wise founders, God's Word, and today's cutting-edge experts is a requirement if you desire to change, grow, and succeed. We do not have to recreate the wheel of success but simply drive along the same paths as other achievers. Now is the time for the self-developer to arise and lay hold to what is not easily given by putting in the hard work that dreams and destiny require.

Pilot Not Co-Pilot

You are the pilot of your Aircraft Self-Development. You are not the Co-Pilot. Co-pilot is for salvation, servant leadership, and other concepts but not for your development, change, and success. You must, and I say again, rely more on self-development than other greatness development principle to achieve a stable structured environment and success path for the new you. It is most beneficial to put in the leg work yourself to achieve success at any level of change rather than to expect success to be spoon-fed to you through the efforts and care of others. Sure, others will provide you with opportunities and access to promotion and success but please be sure not to get the two confused with what is necessary for you to grow and achieve destiny. There is absolutely no one to blame for your lack of structure or success in any new experience other than self. On the flip side there is no one responsible for it but self either. Self-development is simply investing adequate time and learning into your knowledge, spirituality, skills, psychology, education, and mastery. Contrary to overzealous religion, we are responsible for self-development. It was never God's idea to do all the work while we become lazy throughout the process.

History proves from most experts in the industry of Success and

Self-Development that you can grow your success and productivity times one thousand when you consistently practice self-development principles. Dr. David J. Schwartz, in his book The Magic of Thinking Big wrote, *"Normally, people think of investing in terms of stocks or bonds, real estate, or some other type of property. But the biggest and most rewarding kind of investment is self-investment, purchasing things which build mental power and proficiency."* Your life and everything and everyone around you will change and get better when you change and get better. It is just an act of nature. Your positive energy and influence will spill over like running lava. It will spread like an abundant grape vine and influence the attitudes and behaviors of others. There is no stopping the force of energy that leaps off of positive effort like your personal development. Here is a road map to get you started. Maybe it is a refresher. There may be one or two concepts mentioned that you find more rewarding than others. Practice them and you will grow into your greatness. Let's begin with the Law of Belief. I actually covered this one in the previous chapters. However, it's so powerful that it is worth revisiting.

The Law of Belief

Belief is essential to your life success and the changes that you desire to initiate or endure. Whatever you believe will come to pass. Your thought life is the key to achievement or the lack thereof. When you focus on negativity, you attract it. When you focus on positive outcomes and expect great things, you will benefit from those beliefs. The key is emotion and faith. The Law of Belief, a psychology principle that is also associated with success, says that whatever you believe with feelings becomes your reality. You can create a new reality or outcome with your believing thoughts. How? Your thoughts drive your emotions and actions. Your believing thoughts move God to act on your behalf. You often do or do not do what you think or do not think. In the New Testament book of Matthew 9:27-29, the author discusses a story where two blind men approached Jesus Christ of Nazareth requesting that He heal them.

Jesus' immediate response to the blind men was, "Do you believe that I am able to do this?" The focus here was on their belief system. Jesus was feeding them knowledge of what could be. He knew the Law of Belief.

The two blind men responded, "Yes, Lord." Jesus then touched their eyes saying, "According to your faith let it be for you." Whatever you believe with emotion and faith, sets the tone for what can happen in your life. Remember the Law of Belief. Practice it daily. Use your mind to tune up the success of your goals, dreams, change, growth, and destiny.

Self-Discipline

Without self-discipline you are stuck dead in the water. You are like a man sinking in quicksand. You will be like the Children of Israel in the Book of Exodus who kept repeating the same journey around Mt. Sinai because they repeated the same mistakes over and over again. Without self-discipline you will repeat the same mistakes over and over again. Your level of knowledge, professionalism, wealth, influence, skill, or anything else will not do much good if you lack the self-discipline necessary to put them to significant use repeatedly. Self-discipline is the act of doing what is needed when it is needed. It is the science of knowing the right information and the art of applying it at the appropriate time. Practicing self-discipline means that you are willing to give up whatever it takes to achieve your goals, dreams, change, growth, and success. Leave out self-discipline and you will fail. Employ that practice of it and you will succeed. The difference between success and failure is the inability to act repeatedly. Begin training yourself to deny immediate gratification and watch how you prosper. Self-discipline is self-control on display. It keeps you in check and away from the harm you can cause yourself. The key here is you. Apply self-discipline everywhere in your life. Farm your life by cultivating and fertilizing the ground of your endeavors with self-discipline. Darren Hardy once said, "The key to success is no longer information it's action."

Coaching and Mentoring

I cannot say enough about the benefits and power of having a coach or mentor. Coaching as well as mentoring is the science and art of interpersonal development by interdependence with another. In other words, the two are all about intimate relationships that are built on vulnerability, trust, and accountability. You should never attempt greatness alone. No man has and succeeds. Ecclesiastes 4:9-12 (AMP) reveals, *"Two are better than one because they have a more satisfying return for their labor; for if either of them falls, the one will lift up his companion. But woe to him who is alone when he falls and does not have another to lift him up. Again, if two lie down together, then they keep warm; but how can one be warm alone?*

And though one can overpower him who is alone, two can resist him. A cord of three strands is not quickly broken."

Successful people understand the value of gleaning and learning, even grooming from the high-achievers and wise sages who have gone before them. If you do not have a coach, mentor, or at least employ the services of one or the other throughout your lifetime, you are alone. As a matter of fact, your worth and value is limited without the rich insight, wisdom, and knowledge of others being poured into you. The more knowledge and wisdom you gain, the higher your profitability potential. The more you grow internally, mentally, psychologically, spiritually, and emotionally the greater your worth. One coaching or mentoring session can raise your productivity and potential by one thousand percent. As a matter of fact, I have mentored and coached clients whose lives I have seen dramatically change for good. They were stuck dead in the water until they employed my services.

A coach is someone with proven skills and competencies in the industry who can transfer them into an authentic relationship with you. A coach uses expert listening skills, keen awareness, powerful questions, discovery concepts, strategic planning, and a rich sense of communication to help you draw out the best that is in you. He or she is just that – a coach. A coach is not a counselor. Counselors help you relive the past to heal and direct your emotions, thoughts, and behaviors successfully in the present and future. A coach begins with your present and partners with you to navigate your present into your future successfully-only with your permission. A mentor is a guide or an example of success. Mentors are for disciples. With mentoring your role as a mentee is to learn what the mentor does, learn his/her philosophies, adapt their life, or career psychology and put those things into practice. Unlike a coach, mentors give instructions. They ask questions; however, their power is in pointing you in the right direction. They are role models at best. You need a coach or mentor for every area of life. Your relationships, career, finances, reference groups, spirituality, etc. will flourish abundantly with the help of a mentor and coach. When you want to be successful, you will invest and pay the small price for great growth and success. Most people want something for free or cheap, so they bypass the value of a coach or mentor. Well, you get what you pay for. When you fail to see the value in paying for success, it will elude you. Get a mentor or a coach.

Power of Positive Thinking

Positive thinking is powerfully connected to finding happiness and contentment in every area of life. The more positive that you are in your thoughts toward yourself and others, the more success you will see. Positive reinforcement is necessary to help you weather the trouble and adversities that you will experience on your journey to growth, success, change, destiny, and purpose. The Law of Substitution suggests that your mind can only hold one thought at a time. You can substitute any thought at any time good or bad. You are in control of what you think. If you have a negative thought in your mind, you can simply substitute it with a positive thought.

You do not have to settle for what is called "stinking thinking." You can train your mind to focus on the good and fruitful thoughts that move you toward your success and dreams. The Bible teaches this concept as well. Philippians 4:8 (AMP) says, *"Finally, believers, whatever is true, whatever is honorable and worthy of respect, whatever is right and confirmed by God's word, whatever is pure and wholesome, whatever is lovely and brings peace, whatever is admirable and of good repute; if there is any excellence, if there is anything worthy of praise, think continually on these things [center your mind on them, and implant them in your heart]."*

Psychologists and success mentors believe that a key to positive thinking is a concept called "self-talk." If you recall, we have discussed self-talk at length in previous chapters. Self-talk is the practice of positive self-encouragement. It is designed to create enthusiasm, excitement, and positive energy necessary to keep you on track with your goals, destiny, change, purpose, and success. Positive self-talk includes sayings such as, "I am successful. I am a genuine person. Many like me. I am great at my profession. I am a beautiful person inside and out. I have great success ahead in my future." Practice positive thinking and self-talk every day of your life. It will pay off regardless of what you face. Write personal declarations and decrees that excite you and give you hope. Place them around you in key areas that you visit regularly. Say them to yourself over and over again. Keep your mind focused on the positive in life and not the negative distractions.

Productivity and Peak Performance

We thrive when we are intentional to leap beyond the borders of average into exceptional. The key is to always seek to improve your productivity and performance. One key is adding new skills, new paradigms of thought, and new circles of influence. Only the diligent can achieve this mastery. Bible parables teach that servants have to practice good stewardship of talents and gifts in order to please their employers, etc. Some people are so religious that they fail to identify the additional skills and knowledge necessary to really excel. Others don't care. However, the remaining group are good stewards who understand the value of excellence. When you sacrifice to improve productivity and performance, it pays off. The Bible says in Proverbs 1:5 (AMP), *"The wise will hear and increase their learning, And the person of understanding will acquire wise counsel and the skill [to steer his course wisely and lead others to the truth]."*

Hearing and learning from those at a higher level of expertise and greatness supports the path to personal success. Productivity is your rate of output equal to the rate of expectation. In other words, productivity is the action of being functionally capable of putting out what is expected of you and what you expect of yourself. The idea is to overachieve what is expected of you. Overachievers never settle for average or just for what is expected. They understand that is the way successful people think and act. In order to excel, stand out, get a promotion, achieve the goal, live the life you desire, you must practice excellence. You must learn to run as far from average as possible.

Sometimes being more productive means that you need to practice peak performance. Peak performance is a coaching and success concept designed to help individuals achieve their maximum output and potential in any area of life and career. It requires the process of analyzing strengths, weaknesses, opportunities, and threats in order to streamline activity, manage self, harness energy, unleash skill, develop new habits, and achieve greatness. This process takes time and often solicits the help of others, intense training, and laser focus. However, it does not exclude a life of prayer, servitude, and honor before God. You may have to attend seminars, hire a productivity coach, purchase material, and overhaul your lifestyle. However, it is worth it. Your productivity is why you are hired. Raise it and you will go to the next level of success.

Networking and Master Mind Groups

Your reference group becomes a part of your personality. It is important to have access to other successful people who think and act like you or who are on a level of success and morality higher than yours. Networking and mastermind groups are often essential tools to developing skills and learning new concepts for success. Success comes through sharing life and career journeys with those who can enhance and challenge each level of success and progress that you achieve.

It is necessary to "sharpen the saw" amongst those who have the qualities and motivations to push you and prune you. Success comes with no guarantees. All you have is effort, time, and energy. You need the experiences and wisdom of others to help navigate the challenges and changes that come with pursuing destiny, dreams, and purpose or you may not get there. Networking allows you the opportunity to connect professionally and socially, scale business, and trust others. A mastermind group is one or more persons who can think on your level and share common interests. They can be from the same community, household, industry etc. The idea is to share life and profession with others in a learning environment. Another key focus of mastermind groups is to use mastermind groups to laugh, discuss life, and be yourself. I am sure that you can use more of that. Right?

Practice Core Values

Core values are the unwavering and most important beliefs responsible for your actions, thoughts, and behaviors. They are directly connected to life pursuits and the behavior of achieving those pursuits. Core values are the principles, concepts, and beliefs at the center of our worldview. They are why we are who we are and what you believe. Core beliefs fuel passion, motivation, and desire. Core values are those beliefs that you find most valuable in life. The first step with core values is to identify them. A core belief can be trust, faith, service, success, contribution, significance, family, love, unity, etc. Each of these is a core belief. Once you define what your core beliefs, you will better understand yourself and your life path. Core beliefs keep you on track with what to do and what not to do. They steer you to what attracts your success and away from what detracts from your success. Core beliefs are decision-making tools.

They are why you marry who you marry, live where you live, drive what you drive, and seek what you seek.

There are various processes that you can employ to identify your core values. An important step is to identify why you have a specific core belief. Is it directly connected to your childhood? Are they learned through spiritual or professional growth? Are they genetically a part of your personality? What attributes to that core value? This helps to affirm or weed out your true core values from assumed core values. Core values are not based on a desired response but an actual, present response. You may desire service as a core value. However, you cannot call it a core value if you are not passionate about serving. Identify what is current, then you can work on what is desired.

The self-development tools, resources, and experts are abundantly available to you. All you need is the desire to get better, improve, excel, and be a lifelong student. Then, the teacher will appear. As you tap into these life-changing resources, your internal world will improve and by the Law of Attraction and the Law of Correspondence, your external world will also improve. Jim Rohn said, *"Success is not something that you pursue. It's something you attract."* As much as you may want to brush off the theories, concepts, psychology, strategies, revelations, insights, and facts of this book, the undeniable truth remains that they are right, they work, and they have made others successful. If you apply them with your whole heart, you will be unstoppable at any change, goal, or dream on which your hands are set.

The Journey Ahead

I can promise you that I wrote this book with you in mind. My greatest desire is to serve you and others like you. It is to see you successful. My heart goes out to you with smiles and compassion. My faith goes out to you with expectation and hope. My joy goes out to you with warmth and kindness. I extend my zeal and passion for success to you with intentionality. I would love to know that you are succeeding and found success in this book. I would love to hear from you and to know that something in this book changed your life or prepared you for change, growth, destiny, purpose, and success. I want to see everyone succeed. No one deserves to remain stuck in the same mindset or negative lifestyle. No one deserves to live in remorse and regret. No one deserves to feel like they are unable to cope with life. You cannot give up on yourself, your family, or your dreams. You are amazing even if you do not feel like it. You have greatness in you. Believe this with all of your heart and do your best. If you do not compare yourself to anyone else, you will later see that you can achieve your greatness. Go ahead and be wonderful. Be kind. Be full of grace, wisdom, and mercy. Be supportive. Be successful, innovative, intelligent, charming, and resilient. Be more than you have ever been. The road ahead of you is filled with bumps, pitfalls, potholes, traps, predators, toxins, and more. At the same time, it is filled with new friends, opportunities, promotions, destiny, grace, laughter, blessings, surprises, love, enchantment, and more. Embrace them all as best you can. They are all trainers. Learn from them. Learn the path of contentment and you will find hope in every situation. The journey ahead is what you make of it.

Remember, you are a beautiful butterfly in the making. Wherever you are in life, those days will soon be over. When you make the mental shift from pre-contemplation and take the journey into action, you will feel so much better about life. You will witness a complete transformation in your character, discipline, conversation, mentality, emotions, and success. There is nothing and no one able to stop you now. You are equipped for every change that will ever happen in your life – good or bad. Focus on these principles. Digest them. Meditate on them. You will find the truth in each of these principles if you look for it. I have lived and experienced each of these principles over and over again because change happens over and over again. This is a book that will guide your emotions, behavior, and wisdom at all times. These principles are timeless and have no boundaries. They are applicable to any age demographic, ethnic group, world culture, or corporate endeavor.

The journey ahead is better now. Maybe before reading this book, you felt stuck, powerless, or afraid. Now you have the insight, revelation, confidence, concepts, truths, and more to shake off your chains and go forward. You are equipped with the psychology, biblical support, success concepts, life strategies, and practical tools to excel at change, goals, and greatness. You can conquer anything now. You are not the same person because you have read this book. My most sincere good wishes are with you. If no one else is supporting you through well-intended thoughts, prayer, and hope, I am. I am rooting for your best life ever. Now, go be great – Change.

Chapter Conclusions

1. Self-development is the practice of investing in your personal and professional growth through proven strategies and tested wisdom.

2. Who you are and who you could become are trapped or released by your unwillingness or willingness to grow continually?

3. Self-development is the key to transformation, advancement, destiny, purpose, and exponential growth. Self-development has made poor men rich. Self-development has made ignorant men wise. Self-development has birthed innovators of world change and technological advancements. Self-development has produced iconic global leaders and international game-changers.

4. It is most beneficial to put in the leg work yourself to achieve success at any level of change rather than to expect success to be spoon-fed to you through the efforts and care of others.

5. History proves from most experts in the industry of Success and Self-Development that you can grow your success and productivity by one thousand when you consistently practice self-development principles. Dr. David J. Schwartz, in his book The Magic of Thinking Big wrote, *"Normally, people think of investing in terms of stocks or bonds, real estate, or some other type of property. But the biggest and most rewarding kind of investment is self-investment, purchasing things which build metal power and proficiency."* (Fireside, 1987)

6. You cannot give up on yourself, your family, or your dreams. You are amazing even if you do not feel like you are. Just know that you are! Believe this with all of your heart and do your best. If you do not compare yourself to anyone else, you will achieve greatness.

7. Remember, you are a beautiful butterfly in the making. Wherever you are in life, those days will soon be over. When you make the mental shift from pre-contemplation and take the journey into action, you will feel so much better about life.

About the Author

D<small>r.</small> Jerrell Stokley, Jr.is professionally known in the Coaching and Entrepreneurial industry as "Coach." He credits the Lord's grace for his life and success. He overcame childhood depression, abuse, death of fiancé,' and poverty. As a young adult he was blessed to overcome the murder of his former fiancé,' homelessness, and a sinister six – year custody battle for his sons. He later overcame a brain tumor, as well as business and personal loss. His transformation continues to lead to his successes. Dr. Stokley teaches, motivates, and encourages others to succeed in transformational ways through spiritual renewal, success psychology, peak performance, Grit, and self-development.

Jerrell T. Stokley, Jr.is a seasoned and dynamic Speaker, Influencer, and Trainer. He has successfully evolved, by the grace of God, into a Church Planter, Author, Coach and Entrepreneur. He has nearly thirty years of leadership experience transforming lives and training leaders. Currently, he is the President/Managing Member of Glory Gear LLC, Founder/ President of Covenant Grace, Founder/CEO of Jerrell Stokley Ministries, President/Managing Member of Stokley Enterprises, CEO/Managing Member of Jerrell Stokely LLC, whose services include Maximum Success Coaching, Maximum Success Academy, and Proverbs 27 Group.

Jerrell T. Stokley, Jr. holds a Doctor of Education in Leadership, Master of Divinity, Master of Organizational Leadership & Coaching, and Bachelor of Religion. He is an ICF Coach Member, Leadership Coach, and Certified Executive Coach. He has written and published several books including Born to Overcome, No Pain, No Purpose; The Search, *Six Dimensions of Purpose*; Becoming Your Best You, Looking Within, Redefining the Christian Leader in You. He has been married to his supportive wife, Angela Stokley, for nearly thirty years. He is also the father of a blended family of four beautiful children.

To book Dr. Stokley for coaching and consulting services, motivational speaking, leadership training, Coach Certification, or the ministry of preaching, please contact Stokley Enterprises at 1-888-885-8232. Visit www.JerrellStokley.com, www.maximumsuccesscoaching.com, www.JerrellStokleyMinistries.org, and www.CovenantGraceChurch.org, for a life-changing connection with Dr. Jerrell T. Stokley, Jr.

Bibliography

1. Amplified Bible (AMP) Copyright © 2015 by The Lockman Foundation, La Habra, CA 90631. All rights reserved.
2. Branden, Nathaniel. *The Six Pillars of Self-Esteem*. New York: Bantam, 1994.
3. BrainyQuote.com. Xplore Inc., 2016. 13 May 2016. http://www.brainyquote.com
4. Carnegie, Dale. *How to Win Friends and Influence People*. New York: Simon and Schuster, 1981.
5. Chand, Samuel R. *Failure: The Womb of Success*. Niles: Mall Publishing Co, 1969.
6. Cialdini, Robert B. *Influence: The Psychology of Persuasion*. New York: Collins, 2007.
7. Clason, George S. *The Richest Man in Babylon*. New York: Hawthorn, 1955.
8. Collin, Catherine. *The Psychology Book*. New York: DK Pub, 2012.
9. Collins, James C. *Good to Great: Why Some Companies Make the Leap ... and Others Don't*. New York: Harper Business, 2001.
10. Covey, Stephen R. *The Seven Habits of Highly Effective People: Restoring the Character Ethic*. New York: Simon and Schuster, 1989.
11. Dollar, Creflo A. *8 Steps to Create the Life You Want: The Anatomy of a Successful Life*. New York: Faith Words, 2008.
12. Flaherty, James. *Coaching: Evoking Excellence in Others*. Boston: Butterworth-Heinemann, 1999.
13. Gensler, Harry J. *Ethics: A Contemporary Introduction*. New York: Routledge, 2011.
14. Hackman, Michael Z, and Craig E. Johnson. *Leadership: A Communication Perspective*. Long Grove: Waveland Press, 2004.

15. Hardy, Darren. *The Compound Effect: Multiplying Your Success, One Simple Step at a Time*. New York: Vanguard Press, 2010.

16. Hill, Napoleon, Joe Slattery, and W C. Stone. *Think & Grow Rich*. Arden: Highroads Media, 2003.

17. Jakes, T D. *Destiny: Step into Your Purpose*. N.p., 2015.

18. Jakes, T D. *Instinct: The Power to Unleash Your Inborn Drive*. N.p., 2014.

19. Jakes, T D. *Reposition Yourself: Living Life Without Limits*. New York: Atria Books, 2007.

20. Jakes, T D. *Reposition Yourself: [living Life Without Limits]*. New York: Simon & Schuster Audio, 2007.

21. Kiyosaki, Robert T, and Sharon L. Letcher. *Rich Dad, Poor Dad: What the Rich Teach Their Kids About Money That the Poor and Middle Class Do Not!* N.p., 2000.

22. Lapin, Daniel. *Thou Shall Prosper: Ten Commandments for Making Money*. Hoboken, N.J: John Wiley & Sons, 2010.

23. Malphurs, Aubrey. *Being Leaders: The Nature of Authentic Christian Leadership*. Grand Rapids: Baker Books, 2003.

24. Malphurs, Aubrey, and Will Mancini. *Building Leaders: Blueprints for Developing Leadership at Every Level of Your Church*. Grand Rapids: Baker Books, 2004.

25. Munroe, Myles. *In Pursuit of Purpose*. Shippensburg: Destiny Image, 1992.

26. Munroe, Myles. *Overcoming Crisis: The Secrets to Thriving in Challenging Times*. Shippensburg: Destiny Image Pub, 2009.

27. Munroe, Myles. *The Principles and Benefits of Change: Fulfilling Your Purpose in Unsettled Times*. New Kensington: Whitaker House, 2009.

28. Munroe, Myles. *The Principles and Power of Vision*. New Kensington: Whitaker House, 2003.

29. Munroe, Myles. *Understanding Your Potential*. Shippensburg: Destiny Image Publishers, 1991.

30. Ramsey, Dave. *Entreleadership: 20 Years of Practical Business Wisdom from the Trenches*. New York: Howard Books, 2011.

31. Ries, Al, and Jack Trout. *The 22 Immutable Laws of Marketing: Violate Them at Your Own Risk*. New York: Harper Business, 1993.

32. Rohn, Jim, E J. Rohn, and Chris Widener. *Twelve Pillars: A Novel*. Irving: Jim Rohn International and Chris Widener International, 2005.

33. Schwartz, David J. *The Magic of Thinking Big*. New York: Simon & Schuster, 1987.

34. Stanley, Andy. *Visioneering*. Sisters: Multnomah Publishers, 1999.

35. Stoltzfus, Tony. *Leadership Coaching: The Disciplines, Skills, and Heart of a Coach*. Virginia Beach: T. Stoltzfus, 2005.

36. *The New International Webster's Pocket Business Dictionary of the English Language*. Naples: Trident Press International, 1998.

37. The Three Types of Intelligence You Need for Success, https://www.psychologytoday.com/blog/cutting-edge-leadership/201310/the-three-types-intelligence-you-need-success, Oct. 7, 2013. Ronald E. Riggio, Ph.D., is the Henry R. Kravis Professor of Leadership and Organizational Psychology and former Director of the Kravis Leadership Institute at Claremont McKenna College.

38. Tracy, Brian. *No Excuses! The Power of Self-Discipline*. New York: Vanguard Press, 2010.

39. Wikipedia contributors. "Alfred Nobel." Wikipedia, The Free Encyclopedia. Wikipedia, The Free Encyclopedia, 3 May. 2016. Web. 14 May. 201

40. Willard, Dallas, and Don Simpson. *Revolution of Character: Discovering Christ's Pattern for Spiritual Transformation*. Colorado Springs, CO: NavPress, 2005

41. www.cpe.vt.edu/gttc/presentations/8eStagesofChange.pdf. Retrieved May 5, 2016

42. www.wisdomquotes.com. Retrieved May 26, 2016

Printed in the United States
by Baker & Taylor Publisher Services